7 STEPS TO GREATNESS

The Masterplan to Take Your Life, Studies,
Career and Business to the Next Level

Dr Patrick Businge

Published by Greatness University Publishers
www.greatness-university.com

ISBN 978-1-9999494-0-2
ISBN 1999949404

DEDICATION

This book is dedicated to you. You have something special. There is greatness within you. May the 7 steps help you unleash the greatness in you.

CONTENTS

ACKNOWLEDGEMENTS

This masterplan would have not been possible without the mentoring of Les Brown: world's number one motivational speaker, Ona Brown: expert in personal transformation, Brian Tracy: bestselling author and world's top success coach, and Omar Periu: world leading wealth coach. I was also fortunate to come to the attention of Antonio Smith Jr, Founder of Plant Better University who wrote the forward.

I am indebted to colleagues in the Les Brown Maximum Achievement Team, Brian Tracy's Mastermind Group, and to Greatness University Maximum Achievement Team. It is because of their critical friendship and social and moral support that I have accomplished writing this masterplan.

Special thanks to my family, relatives and friends. While my father Mr George Rusoke inspired my head, my mother Stella Rusoke ignited my heart. I cannot fail to thank my wife Mrs Julian Businge and my two little children for the patience and courtesy I received whilst writing this book. Special applause to Mr Paul Padde who proofread my manuscript. I cannot end without mentioning all my students and the great people from all over the world who have inspired me and shaped my thinking in this book.

PREFACE

I first met Dr Patrick Businge at an event in Florida. Les Brown, the world's number 1 motivational speaker and our mentor, headlined the event. When I shared the stage with Patrick and listened to his message, I instantly knew there was something very special about him. Obviously, my gut feeling was correct. As if he was reading my mind, he introduced himself to me and I was introduced to the man behind the talent.

A few months later, the calm and mild-mannered man with a sweet accent asked me to write a preface to his book. I agreed immediately. How could I resist honouring such an honourable figure after seeing people fall in love with his message in Florida? Patrick is a wonderful person who has managed to write one of the most practical books on self-help I have read in a long time. Follow his message and your life will be transformed.

This book is simply extraordinary largely because of the way life has wired Dr Patrick Businge. His mind is saturated with universal truth. As you will discover in each chapter, he is passionate, sometimes to a fault, about being effective for greatness. I doubt if there is a person on the planet who knows both universal laws on greatness as well as practical application in depth as Dr Patrick Businge. This combination is at times mind-boggling.

Dr Patrick Businge is both the messenger and message of greatness in this book. From many interactions with him as a teacher, colleague and friend, my judgment is this: Dr Patrick Businge is a prosperous mind that keeps pace with the best. Almost without fail, a conversation with him will fill you with knowledge that surpasses all understanding. So, I am happy to entice all kinds of people to this book. If I must, I will visit your house and become a door-to-door salesman and entice you to this book.

We all need a path to greatness and Dr Patrick Businge has provided one of the very best. May life be kind to all who read the '7 Steps to Greatness' for the wings of prosperity are tucked within, and they have no respect of person. If you want to fly, your wings and passport to any destination you desire will be found within this book. I love you all.

Antonio T. Smith, Jr, Bestselling author of *Keep Walking*

CALLED TO GREATNESS

'Though no one can go back and make a brand new start, anyone can start from now and make a brand new ending'. Attributed to Carl Bard

Most people want to be successful in their careers and studies. They want to create businesses, have meaningful relationships and make a difference to their loved ones. Like skilled architects, people want to design their lives beautifully and leave a legacy. Indeed, people want to achieve their goals and live a great life. However, most people rarely have a plan to make this happen. They do not know what they need to build a meaningful and successful life. They are unaware of the steps to take from where they are to where they want to be. I believe this is because they never ask life-changing questions such as these. Who am I? Why am I alive today? I am living my dreams or my fears? What are my goals and plans? Am I seeing my dreams and goals becoming true? What are the kind of people I associate with? What actions am I taking to live a great life?

You may have already answered these questions. You know who you are. You know your life's purpose. You are living a life of your wildest dreams. You have set yourself goals and have achieved them. You are already living a great life and nothing needs to change. If this is happening for you, well done. You are one in a million. You have already stepped into your greatness.

If you have not yet stepped into your greatness, then this book is for you. The world's number one motivational speaker Les Brown says, 'Greatness is a choice not a destiny'. Like most people, you may not be aware that you have to choose to be great. Given that most people do not ask these life changing questions, given that most people do not choose to be great, they die without manifesting their greatness. They leave this planet with their greatness unused. That is why Les Brown says, 'The graveyard is the richest place on earth, because it is here that you will find all the hopes and dreams that were never fulfilled, the books that were never written, the songs that were never sung, the inventions that were never shared, the cures that were never discovered, all because someone was too afraid to take that first step, keep with the problem, or determined to carry out their dream'.

This book is written for people who have the courage to follow their heart and step into their greatness. It is a masterplan for those who want to take the road less travelled and live full. It is inspired by what I have experienced as I travelled to various parts of the world and lived among various great people. It is informed by what I have learnt from my mother who lived in poverty but did not allow poverty to live in her. It is informed by what I have learnt from my father who was imprisoned because of his dream to educate me. So, the 7 steps in this book are not hypothetical but are based on the journey I have taken from a being missionary to a parent, from a student to teacher, from author to an international speaker, from a migrant worker to a successful entrepreneur in the United Kingdom.

The content of this book is also based on the many years of research and unrivalled mentoring I have received. Learning from my parents that freedom from ignorance is greater that freedom from prison, I have been mentored by the best and the brightest including Les Brown: world's number one motivational speaker, Ona Brown: expert in personal transformation, Brian Tracy: bestselling author and world's top success coach, Omar Periu: self-made millionaire and world leading wealth coach, and Brahm Norwich: Professor of education. I have read widely from great people in the field of personal development such as Robin Sharma:

leadership expert, Mike Williams: business strategist, and Tony Robins: world's top life coach.

My mentors and other great people have helped millions of people live their dreams and not their fears. I have condensed all that I have learnt from them to date in this masterplan which I am sharing with you because I believe in you and in your dreams. I believe in your potential to take your life, business, studies, career to the next level and live a great life. Now is time to step into your greatness.

It is often said that the first step is always the hardest. In the first step to greatness, I am sending you on a mission to search and find yourself. Who are you? What is at the core of your being? What makes you 'you'? Where have you been with your life? Once you have found yourself, you are given a special gift that contains your greatness. With this gift, your life is to take on a new meaning and your eyes are to open to see a new horizon. But you are not stopping here. You are going to take the next step.

In the second step to greatness, I am inviting you to discover your purpose in this immense universe. I am challenging you to answer the following questions: why are you alive today? What has brought you to this planet? What is your burning desire? What is your personal mission? How are the future generations to know that your life was worth living? What is the vision for your life? What inspires you to get into action, be in action, and stay in action? Once you discover your purpose, you are to guard it like the apple of your eye. But you are not stopping here. You are climbing to the next step.

In the third step to greatness, I will volunteer to be your midwife. If you allow me, I will help you and your purpose give birth to your wildest dreams. I will also invite you to take the advice from the famous actor James Dean and 'dream as if you will live forever'. I will challenge you to dream while you are awake. You will be intrigued to dream big because you probably know from the author of *As a Man Thinketh*, James Allen, that 'dreamers are the saviours of the world'. The big dreams you have will push you out of your comfort zone and you will witness defining moments unfold in your life. With this zeal and motivation, you will not stop here. You will crave to climb the next step.

Benjamin E Mays, American civil rights activist and spiritual mentor to Martin Luther King Jr, says, 'The tragedy of life doesn't lie in not reaching your goal. The tragedy lies in having no goal to reach'. So, in the fourth step to greatness, you are going to learn the importance of having goals. You are going to be introduced to S.T.A.R© goals. You are invited to have goals that are strongly felt in your heart and are connected to your dreams. You are able to visualise these goals in the theatre of your mind. Your goals are to be absolutely necessary that they become a life and death issue to you. Your goals are going to be difficult to achieve because like Dr Norman Vincent Peale, church minister and author of *The Power of Positive Thinking*, you know that you are shooting for the moon and not the stars. You also understand that when you are stepping into your greatness, the process is more important than the outcome. But you are not stopping here. You are going to be motivated to climb more steps.

In the fifth step to greatness, I am giving you the V.I.S.I.O.N© system as your vehicle to travel to another hemisphere with a different time zone where your dreams are possible. While there, you are going to realise that it is better to live from imagination and not memory. You are going to have the chance to visualise inside your mind with your senses and imagine overcoming obstacles with no fear. The V.I.S.I.O.N© system is going to allow you to have in your mind what you want while knowing, like Napoleon Hill, author and founder of *The Science of Success*, that whatever your mind can conceive and believe, it can achieve. But you are not stopping here. You are climbing further to the next step.

Public speaker and networker Porter Gale gave this title to her book: *Your Network is Your Net Worth*. In the sixth step to greatness, you are going to dedicate your time to reviewing your network using the P.E.O.P.L.E© model. You are going to have the chance to ask these questions about the people you associate with. What are they bringing into my life? Are they purposeful? Are they encouraging? Are they opportunity experts? Are they productive? Are they living full? Are they exemplary? You are going to ask more questions: Do they fuel or empty my life? Do they inspire me to become the best version of me? Do they ignite my heart? Do they empower me? You are going to ask even more and more questions: what am I becoming emotionally, academically, financially, and spiritually because of these people? Upon answering these questions, you are going to attract more great people into your life and repel toxic people from your life. But you are not going to stop here. You are going to take all that you have and all that you are with you to the final step.

Have you ever seen someone standing by the corner of a street? At one point in our life, we are standing at the corner of the street waiting for someone to lead us across. In the seventh step to greatness, you are going to make an unwavering decision and move from the street corner. You are going to refuse to park your life. You are going to follow the incredible A.C.T.I.O.N©. system to finally step into your greatness. The A.C.T.I.O.N© system is going to allow you emulate great people and ask important questions about your life, your dreams, and your goals. You are not going to leave these questions unanswered. You are to embark on the road to educate yourself because you know quality education is food for your mind. You are going to be committed to doing whatever it takes to have what you want.

Reaching the seventh step to greatness is the end of this masterplan but it is not the end of you. It is the end of the 7 steps to greatness but it is not the end of your journey to greatness. You are invited to increase your action as you cruise on the motorway to your greatness forever. And now, it is time for you to start with the first step to greatness. I believe in you. I believe in your dreams. I believe in your potential to live a great life. Let this masterplan be your Satnav to navigate the streets of life. As Satnav is of no use if you keep it in your car boot, so is the knowledge in this book, if not applied. If you do not take action, you will not step into your greatness and live the great life you deserve. I believe that you ready for action. Let us go and take the first step.

STEP 1: Find Yourself

'Once you discover who you are, you have the power to live full and die empty'. Dr Patrick Businge

Thank you for answering the call to greatness and taking the first step. I was like you twenty years ago when I first heard the calling to become a missionary. It involved leaving my native country Uganda and going to work in various places. Though it was exciting for me to travel to different countries in the world, it was startling to face the unknown and embrace other cultures and religions. I vividly remember the first day I arrived in Burkina Faso. Upon arrival at the mission post in the capital city Ouagadougou, I was given a calabash filled with water to drink without asking for it. My kneejerk reaction was 'I do not need water' only to be told that drinking from the calabash was part of the welcoming ceremony.

Like me going to Burkina Faso, you have decided to face the unknown. You have decided to embark on a journey to greatness without knowing what you are going to encounter. I now know something about you. You are very courageous in taking your first step which is often the hardest. Before you continue this journey, I would like to ask you some questions: Where have you been with your life? What have you achieved? Have you ever imagined that your life could be different than it is? What is your deepest desire? What do you really want from life? I would advise you to take time and reflect on these questions.

Life is a question

I once heard a speaker who said, 'life is a question and how you live it is the answer'. This quotation triggered in me a thirst to find the answers to my question: life. I believe you too are searching for answers to your life. Take time and imagine: If you had your life to live over again, how would you live it? Are you ready to change from the person you have been to the person you want to be? I am reminded of a student who entered the classroom talking to his friend while the lesson was about to begin. When the teacher reminded him of the classroom rules, he burst out singing and dancing: 'Don't stop me now I'm having good time'. My question to you is: Are you still having a good time by continuing to live the life you are living now? Imagine how different your life could be if you gave a different answer today.

A quote often attributed to the author Carl Bard says, 'Though no one can go back and make a brand new start, anyone can start from now and make a brand new ending'. Yes! I believe you can have a brand new start to your life as well as a brand new ending. This is possible since you have already answered the call to this unknown and less travelled journey to greatness. Like Les Brown, I believe you are aware that, 'You have to be willing to allow the person you are today to die, so that you can give birth to the person you are meant to become'.

The midwife to a new life

Are YOU ready to give birth to a new 'you'? I can feel the answer inside of you. I would urge you to say it loud: 'I'm ready to give birth to a new life'! As you are now ready to deliver your new life, here is your midwife: deep hunger. You must be hungry for a new 'you'. Deep hunger will help you deliver the life of your dreams. Like you, I have had deep hunger for my dreams. This is my story I would like to share with you.

In Summer 2017, my wife and I were hungry to achieve our dream of becoming international speakers and coaches. Our deep hunger put us on a journey from London in England to Miami in Florida for a life changing mentorship programme with Les Brown - the world's number one motivational speaker. This journey took a lot of time to prepare, a lot of resources and energy from us.

As we travelled via Toronto, we met a lot of amazing people we had never seen before and went through a lot of new places we have never been before. Going through these various 21st Century airports, border posts with cutting age technology and patiently waiting in the mazy queues, I was touched by the questions asked of me and of other passengers by the immigration officers. They would ask: "Who are you? Where have you been? Why are you here? Where are you going? How will you get there? What will you do when you get there?"

Over time, it became clearer that if we wanted to arrive at our destination, we needed to be honest and answer these questions. As you journey to your greatness, as you go through the various border posts in your life, as you patiently queue with a deep hunger to live a great life, I want to ask you these questions too: Who are you? Where have you been with your life? Why are you here today? What has brought you to this planet? Where are you going? How do you see yourself one year from now? In three years? In five years? And, what does the future look like for you? How will you get there? Who will you go with? Will it be your dreams? Your gifts? Your talents? What will you do when you get there?

When my wife and I honestly answered these questions, we were allowed to reach our destination: Florida, The Sunshine State. Today, I want to let you know that when you honestly answer these questions, you will give birth to a new life. You will have access to a new destination and create a brand new ending to your life. It is my wish that reading this book and other *7 Steps to Greatness* resources will allow you to answer these questions with honesty. You will have the chance to explore new territories in your life and answer the life question differently so that you live differently. I believe this is the time to step into yourself and discover the real you. Give it all and decide: 'It is not over until I find myself'.

It is a tragedy

Did you know that most people are not courageous and hungry like you? Let me share with you something that might scare you. Imagine going for a funeral of a very important person in your life. You know the service is today starting at 2pm and you know where the funeral service is going to be. Before the service, everybody is invited to pay their last respects, including you. You approach the coffin and through the glass you look inside. To your surprise, it is you. Imagine - it is YOU! Now ask yourself: If I die today, what would my eulogy look like? How would my close friends describe me? How would my work colleagues remember me? What virtues and qualities would my religious leaders use? What habits will my classmates include? What core beliefs will my family members highlight to the mourners? A quote attributed to one of the founding fathers of the United States of America Benjamin Franklin says, 'Some people die at twenty five and aren't buried until they are seventy five'. Imagine this is true not just for some people but for many people who have already died and are waiting to be buried. What a tragedy!

'It's a tragedy for me to see the dream is over…And I'll never will forget the day we met …' Do you remember this song? It is called 'I'm gonna miss you' by Milli Vanilli. Yes, it is a big tragedy that many people have already left their bodies behind, dying without having taken the time to know themselves and step into their greatness. That is why 'The graveyard is the richest place on earth, because it is here that you will find all the hopes and dreams that were never fulfilled, the books that were never written, the songs that were never sung, the inventions that were never shared, the cures that were never discovered, all because someone was too afraid to take that first step, keep with the problem, or determined to carry out their dream' (Les Brown).

I am sure you do not want to be like them. You desire to be different. You have realised that what you are doing now is only a small fraction of the greatness within you. You can see yourself doing a million times better than now. You do not want to cruise along life guided by your limited experience and desires. You do not want to settle for less. You want to live a life of purpose and so are not satisfied with who you are today. You are craving for a different lifestyle. You want more from life. You are thirsty for a new you.

Know thyself

Over the years, I have come to the realisation that if people want more from life, if they want to make a mark on this planet, if they want to live full and die empty, they must embark on a journey of self-discovery. The ancient Greek philosopher Socrates once said, 'Know thyself for the unexamined life is not worth living'. What a great advice that we need to know ourselves not just on the surface but on a deeper level. In his bestselling book *The Monk Who Sold His Ferrari*, Robin Sharma wrote, 'When you dedicate yourself to transforming your inner world your life quickly shifts from the ordinary into the realm of the extraordinary'. Following the examples of Socrates and Robin Sharma, you might wish to take a journey to your inner world, to your heart of hearts and discover yourself.

Once you know yourself, you will have a chance to live full and die empty. You will develop a deep hunger to make your life a masterpiece because you are a piece of the master. Remember the famous Cherokee saying, 'When you were born, you cried and the world rejoiced. Live your life so that when you die, the world cries and you rejoice'. I am reminded of what I witnessed from 5th December 2013 when Nelson Mandela died at the age of 95. The world cried for Nelson Mandela because he made a lasting contribution as a freedom fighter, moral compass and symbol of the struggle against racial oppression in South Africa.

Sometimes I ask myself, 'What will make the world cry for me when I am gone?' You too might be asking the same question. I might not know you one a personal level as you read this book but I think I know why the world is likely to cry for you. I believe the world will shed tears for you and you will rejoice as you watch these tears because of who you are. You are a miracle child. You are an uncommon person. You are a gifted gift.

You Are a Miracle Child

Have you ever felt that you are miracle? Me, I have. Here is how I discovered that I am a miracle. Follow me on this journey of thought since I would like you to discover yourself in the process. Imagine 'your life' before this life. Yes, I mean it. Your life before the one you are living on this planet. Allow yourself to wonder about the probability of your 'parents to be' ever meeting or falling in love. I am reminded of a story of two people who met at the airport. The lady was travelling to South Africa and the gentleman was going to the United States. The lady's flight was cancelled and as she waited for her next flight, the gentleman started talking to her. That was the beginning of a lifelong marital relationship that ended up in having two children. Had the flight to South Africa not been cancelled, these two children would not have existed.

Now reflect on the circumstances surrounding your coming into this planet. Ponder on the billions of people that live on our planet. Be amazed on how out of more than 40 million sperms, only yours successfully fertilised that egg. Use your imagination and recreate the scene of you being born in the place you were born. The time you were born. The medical personnel that made it possible for a safe delivery. Use your mathematical skills and imagine what some experts say that the probability of you being born is like having 2.5 million people getting together over a game of dice. The 2.5 million people are playing with a special dice with a trillion faces instead of the usual six. Make a calculation and accept that your existence was one in over a trillion chances. Are you not a real miracle? I believe you are a miracle child.

A miracle child

I would like you now to go deeper and feel who you are. The fact that you are still alive and breathing. The fact that you are still here since there are many people you know who are now gone. You too could have been gone a long time ago but you have not. You are still here. As you read this book, think about the fact that it is not up to you to tell your heart to beat so that you continue to be alive. It is not up to you to tell the white blood cells to do what they are needed to do. It is not up to you to command the red blood cells to go where they are meant to go. It is not up to you to instruct your lungs to breathe. It is not up to you to tell your eyes to see the many colours in this world. It is not up to you to instruct your nostrils to smell, your tongue to taste or your brain to think. It is not up to you to fall asleep and wake up alive. All these activities are simultaneously happening regardless of your participation. They are happening regardless of your command. You are not their initiator. At this point, I believe that you are becoming more aware that you are a miracle child.

As a miracle child, you do not have to calculate how much water you need to drink to neutralise the excess salt in your body. From today henceforth, I invite you to become aware that you possess an invisible miracle power that does the calculations automatically without you having to stop. From the day you were conceived, this miracle power continues to solve every problem for you. It repairs your body. It has unlimited power to do everything that you could ever imagine. It is the sole reason you continue to be in this world. This miracle power occupies the whole of your body. It sees without eyes what our eyes have not seen. It hears what our ears have not heard. It communicates without words. This invisible miracle power in you reads your thoughts, experiences your fears, and knows your hopes and your dreams. It is unhindered by distance, by time or by the body. It never dies. It is the most powerful 'thing' in the universe. From it you live, you move and you have your being. Indeed you are a miracle.

On a special mission

There are moments you might not feel you are a miracle. When you run out of finances and you are declared bankrupt. When your health deteriorates and you are told you have few days to live. When your relationship breaks down and what you thought was long-term love becomes lifetime hatred. When you fail your exams and start feeling you are not worthy of success. Even in these moments, you are still a miracle on a special mission.

Now that you are becoming more aware of your miracle power, it is helpful to trust that all the things you desire and all the things you want to create in your life are possible. Your past is approved. Your present is here. Your future is coming. You are committed to fully living your special mission. You are committed to making this world a better place than how you found it. Every day you wake up, you have resolved to leave your average lifestyle behind and you are committed to becoming a better version of yourself. This is your personal and special mission.

The French philosopher Theilhard de Chardin knew it when he said, 'You are a spiritual being immersed in a human experience'. Robert Collier is honest in his book *The Secret of the Ages* by writing, 'You have within you a force against which the whole world is powerless'. One of the foremost spiritual authors Anthony de Mello is sure when he says, 'I have a treasure: the thing that I value most in life. I relive the events that led me to discover it. I think of the history of my life from the time I found this treasure…what it has done and meant to me. I stand before this treasure and I say, "Of all the things I have, you are the dearest"…I am a treasure. Someday, somewhere, someone discovered me. I should have no awareness of my worth if someone had not found it. I recall and relive the details of the finding and I am a multifaceted treasure'. This is the miracle power within you that also makes you uncommon.

You Are Uncommon

Have you ever thought of yourself as an uncommon person? Well, let me start with a short story about the twins. They were born on the same day, in the same hospital and within few minutes of each other. They grew up together, went to the same schools where they studied the same subjects. However, each time they sat for examinations, they achieved different results. When they completed their studies, they went on to create different levels of success, got married to different people and lived differently.

This short story illustrates that, though the twins were similar in many ways, each of them was different and unique. I believe that you too are different irrespective of the common characteristics that you share with other human beings. You are a unique and unrepeatable human being. There is no another 'you' anywhere in this universe. This makes you uncommon and you deserve to live and act in uncommon ways.

The truth is that few people know they are uncommon. The truth is that few people live and act in uncommon ways. In fact, most people have chosen to be common. If they were to sit in the two-tier British Parliament, they would be in the House of Commons rather than in the House of Lords. Look at it this way, the few Lords are the uncommon people selected on merit, based on their contributions to the British society while those in the Commons are voted into parliament by the masses, based on their power of persuasion.

Take time to reflect on your life now. If you were allowed to sit in the British Parliament, where would you go? The House of Lords or the House of Commons? As you continue discover the miracle power within you, there is nothing to stop you from being uncommon. You are not going to settle for a common and average life after knowing that you have an immense miracle power within you that makes you unique.

From today forth, I would like you to know that you are uncommon. You deserve to sit in the House of Lords. You are unique and unrepeatable. There is no one else anywhere like you. It is possible for you to live an uncommon life. Now that you know you are uncommon, I urge you to bypass your eyesight and tap into your mindsight and heartsight.

One of my favourite books contains a story of Moses who used his mindsight to bypass his eyesight. With his eyesight, he saw a burning bush that was on fire. With his mindsight he came to the conclusion that this bush which was on fire without burning was an uncommon bush. With his heartsight, he was not frightened by the bush but went closer to discern why this was the case. It is during this moment that Moses discovered the miracle power behind the burning bush. What a transition from eyesight to mindsight to heartsight.

The burning bush inside you

You might find it helpful to reflect on these questions. How often do you use your mindsight and heartsight? Have you found the bush within you that is on fire? What about the miracle power beyond that bush burning within you? For Moses, beyond the bush was someone special calling him to live an uncommon life. This uncommon calling required Moses to perform uncommon actions and say uncommon words.

I hope your response to the miracle power within you will be as uncommon as that given by Moses. Your response to the calling will be as uncommon as the calling. Remember, no one in this universe is going to experience life in the same way as you are experiencing it. You are who you are today because of the decisions you have made in your past. Refuse to allow your past struggles and failures become your standard. If you wish to make this transition, I would encourage you to make three decisions today and change your life. Start bypassing your eyesight and find the burning bush inside you. Next, use your mindsight to listen to the bush within you as it rustles while it burns. Last, follow your heartsight to go beyond the bush and live an uncommon life.

Beyond the statue

I know it is possible for you to live an uncommon life. While I was writing this book, I sought advice from my mentor Brian Tracy on how to write a great book. He advised me that in order to be a great writer, I needed to be a good reader. So, I embarked on searching and reading great books. In my search, I came across John Mason's book titled *You're Born an Original Don't Die a Copy*. From this title, I was led to reflect on the extent to which I was living my life as an original. I then read books written by the foremost spiritual guru Anthony de Mello. I was moved by his reflection on the statue that I would like to share with you:

A sculptor has been making a statue of you. The statue is ready and you go to his studio to have a look at it before it appears in public. He gives you the key to the room where your statue is so that you can see it for yourself and take all the time you want to examine it alone.

You open the door. The room is dark. There, in the middle of the room is your statue, covered with a cloth... You walk up to the statue and take the cloth off...Then you step back and look at your statue. What is your first impression?...Are you pleased or dissatisfied?...Notice the material it is made of...Walk around it...see it from different angles...Look at it from far, then come closer and look at the details...Touch the statue... notice whether it is rough or smooth... cold or warm to the touch. What parts of the statue do you like?...What parts of the statue do you dislike?...

Say something to your statue...What does the statue reply?...What do you say in return?...What do you say in return? Keep on speaking as long as you or the statue have something to say...Now become the statue...What does it feel like to be your statue?…What kind of existence do you have as the statue?'

Reading John Mason and Anthony de Mello's books have led me to question what kind of existence I am living: as a copy? Statue? Original? After reading and reflecting on this, you too might be moved to question yourself. You may be feeling like the co-founder of Apple Steve Jobs who said, 'For most of my life, I've felt that there must be more to our existence than meets the eye. This is who I am, and you can't expect me to be someone I'm not'. From this, you and I get the idea that life could be different for us if we decided to go beyond ourselves, beyond our bodies, and beyond our statues. This is only possible if we access the miracle power within us.

I believe that the universe is eagerly waiting for you to go beyond your statue. It is begging you to live an uncommon life and manifest your greatness. To make this happen, here are some of the things you might consider doing. Educate yourself every day because knowledge is the new currency. Read daily because you know reading is food for the mind. See differently because you not only have eyesight but also mindsight and heartsight. With your mindsight, focus on what is going on in the stadium of your mind and not in the football stadiums. With your heartsight, see what is taking place in the theatre of your heart and not in the world's famous auditoriums.

When you do this, you will live differently. You will refuse to be casual about life because you do not want to become a causality. You will hear differently because you are listening to a different voice within you. You will dance differently because you are listening to the beat of a different drum. You will become a light of greatness and leave your mark on the world. You will refuse to be denied because you have not given up on life. You will become unstoppable because you know who you are: someone endowed with various gifts.

You Are a Gifted Gift

So far I have revealed two things to you: You are a miracle in manifestation and you are an uncommon person. This is the last thing I know about you: You are a gift that contains infinite gifts. In most parts of the world, it is customary to receive gifts on special occasions such as birthdays, graduations, and marriages. What gifts have you received on these days? Which one was your greatest gift?

I would like to reveal to you one of your greatest gifts: This gift is YOU. I believe you are the gift. The famous theologian Hans Urs von Balthasar says it best: 'What you are is God's gift to you, what you become is your gift to God'. What a cherished gift you are. This might be unsettling if you do not believe in God. Let me rephrase it for you: Your life is a gift and how you live it is a gift. At this point, there is no need to know where this gift comes from or to whom this gift goes to. What is important is to believe that you are a gift. What kind of gift are you?

Discover your gifts

To discover yourself as a gift, take time and reflect on these questions: What have I been doing with my life? Do I love it? What is my heart telling me now? Where do my interests lie? What do I like most? What do I excel in? What do I desire to do with my life? I encourage you to take time and discover yourself as a gifted gift. You are a gift that contains many other gifts. With the myriad of gifts you have, you will achieve far beyond your horizons in avenues of life you have never explored. With these innumerable gifts, you will go to many places that you could ever imagine.

Brilliant and accomplished individuals such as the great composer Wolfgang Amadeus Mozart, the great inventor Thomas Edison, and the professional basketball player Michael Jordon, just to name a few, used their gifts to take their lives to new horizons. Holy men and women like St Theresa of Avila, St Julian of Norwich, and St Teresa of Calcutta followed the Holy Spirit to live their spiritual greatness. You too are invited to be on this journey. Work towards becoming a gift that the world will be proud to have. This is your way of thanking the universe for the lovely home you have been living in. This is your way of thanking the universe for taking care of you. Do not deprive the universe from seeing your gifts.

The greatest gift

You know you have many gifts. Can you guess what your greatest gift is? Do you remember the miracle power within you? Robert Collier in his book *Secret of the Ages* writes, 'Always there is something within you urging you on to bigger things, giving you no peace, no rest, no chance to be lazy…This "something" within you keeps telling you that you can do anything you want to do, be anything you want to be, have anything you want to have…'. Kurt Hahn, educator and founder of Outward Bound, once said, 'There is more in us that we know. If we can be made to see it, perhaps, for the rest of our lives, we will be unwilling to settle for less'. Then, the motivational speaker Les Brown says, 'You have something special, you have greatness within you'.

'Something within you' is your greatest gift. 'The more in you' is your greatest gift. The 'Greatness within you' is your greatest gift.

I believe your greatness is patiently waiting for you to discover it. The more in you wants to be used and not expire with you. It would be a pity if you reached the end of your life only to discover that you have used only three percent of your greatness. The American philosopher Henry David Thoreau captures this best when he says: 'Oh, God, to reach a point of death only to realise that you have never lived'. Can you imagine reaching at the end of your life only to discover that you are dying without using your greatness, without tapping into the more in you, without discovering 'something within you'! Make a resolute decision to live full so that you may die empty. Allow life to use you so that you are able to share your gifts with the world. As St Teresa of Calcutta would say, become a pencil in the hand of God and write a new chapter with your life every day.

Your gift of greatness has the potential to allow you live your greatest life. You can get all that you want in any area of your life if you tap into this gift of greatness. People who do not know the value of their greatness are easy prey. I am reminded of President Jomo Kenyatta in his book Facing Mount Kenya where he writes, 'When the missionaries arrived, the Africans had the land and the missionaries had the Bible. They taught us how to pray with eyes closed. When we opened them, they had the land and we had the Bible'. These people in Africa had a treasure in their hands but they did not know it. They did not use it. However, the missionaries knew it, and used it. This is the situation that some of us are in. Greatness is a fortune that we all possess. We should never let it be stolen from us by our limited vision of who we are. Let nobody, let no circumstance or anything steal your greatness from you.

Look beyond your fears

Most people are not living their greatness because they do not see beyond the horizons of their problems. Anger, frustration, fear, guilt, unhappiness, and resentment often slows down our pace to greatness. These emotions are daily killers and can steal our life from us, making us mentally and physically ill. They require us to be brave and act in spite of our fears.

I am sure that you are not prepared to dwell on your fears forever. I used to but this changed when I met Les Brown. I remember listening to him telling a story of a man who was afraid of a dog in his neighbourhood. Whenever he would pass, the dog would bark and he would run away. One day he decided to face his fear and developed the courage to face the dog. The dog came towards him and he did not run. When the dog reached him, he grabbed it by the collar only to realise it had no teeth. Wow! All those times this man had been running from this dog - it had no teeth! I encourage you to take courage and face your fears. Like the dog, your fears might not have any teeth. Grab your fears by the collar and show them you are unstoppable. Show them you have miracle power within you. Do not let your fears obscure the steps to your greatness.

At this point, I am reminded of my numerous journeys to Rome every year over the past 5 years. Each time I go, I climb over 500 steps to the top of St Peter's Basilica. What has surprised me over the years is that each time I climb to the top, I meet people on the way conquering their fear of heights. Once they reach the top they are happy to see the beautiful horizon.

The truth is, not everyone who climbs to the top of St Peter's Basilica, sees a new horizon. The truth is that not everyone who climbs to the top of the Eiffel Tower or the London Eye, challenge themselves to see far. The reality is that we live in a world where most people are prisoners to their comfort zones.

As you step into your greatness, I encourage you to decrease your fears and increase your hope. This will permit you to look beyond the horizon of your struggles. There you will see a beautiful vista which will inspire you to be a 'no matter what person'. With this determination, you will be able to achieve far beyond your limited horizons. You will have the power to walk in the avenues of life that you have never explored. In his book *Secret of the Ages*, Robert Collier writes, 'The power to be what you want to be, to get what you desire, to accomplish whatever you are striving for, abides within you. It rests with you only to bring it forth and put it to work'.

It is a fact that many people who would have wished to read this book and step into their greatness have already gone before you. Given the fact that you are still alive and breathing, you are here waiting to accomplish a special mission. It is necessary that you walk every day towards accomplishing 'the more in you'. I believe you can do everything with the greatness within you. Decide to become unstoppable in the pursuit of your greatest life.

Final Reflection

Now that you have come to the end of this first step, it is time to reflect on the special gift you are. I believe you have discovered more about who you are now than before you read this book. With this self-knowledge, your life is taking on a new meaning and your eyes are opening to new horizons. Even if you forgot most of what you read, you still know that you are a miracle child, you are an uncommon person, and you are a gift with many gifts. In short, this is the **MUG** (Miracle Uncommon Gift) of greatness I am giving you to take with you to the next step.

Now that you have your MUG of greatness, you have the power to live your dreams. Remember 'The graveyard is the richest place on earth, because it is here that you will find all the hopes and dreams that were never fulfilled, the books that were never written, the songs that were never sung, the inventions that were never shared, the cures that were never discovered, all because someone was too afraid to take that first step, keep with the problem, or determined to carry out their dream' (Les Brown).

Now that you have your MUG of greatness, you have the courage to live full and die empty. The ancient Greek philosopher Socrates says, 'Know thyself for the unexamined life is not worth living'. My advice to you is to take time and know yourself each day. You are a miracle in action. You are an uncommon person. You are gifted with greatness. Continue to discover yourself as having a MUG of greatness. Use this MUG and all that you have to build your life as a masterpiece because you are a piece from the master.

---

*Before moving on to the next step, complete the activities for **STEP 1** in the accompanying workbook titled '7 Steps to Greatness: The Workbook to Take Your Life, Studies, Career and Business to the Next Level'.*

STEP 2: Discover Your Purpose

'The two most important days in your life are the day
you are born and the day you find out why'.
Mark Twain

I am glad you have taken time to work on yourself and know who you are. You now know that you are a miracle child, you are uncommon and you are a gift with infinite gifts. It is now time for you to use who you are and what you have to get what you want from life. Before you do this, I would like you to imagine a recently discovered country. This country has a lot of untapped resources. You are to organise the delivery of goods and services to your citizens so that your country becomes the most powerful in the world. Before you can organise the delivery of goods and services, I would like you to name your country. Which name are you giving it? Do you have any ideas? Are you struggling to find one?

Let me help you out with the most obvious name for your country. This name might be the name you hardly considered. Your country is called 'YOU'. Can you believe it? You are the country with lots of resources. You have a lot of untapped physical, mental, emotional, and spiritual resources. There is more in you than you can ever imagine. There is greatness in you that is waiting for you to unleash it. How are you going to access your resources? In this second step to greatness, I am going to give you the key to access all your unlimited resources.

The pressure within you

Let me start by asking you a question: have you ever driven a car with a flat tyre? This is what usually happens. When one of the front tyres is flat, the car loses balance, slows down, and sways to a wrong direction. When two of the front tyres are flat, the car is often elevated at the back and goes slowly. When all the four tyres are flat, the car is even slower and the tyres makes a lot of noise. It is important to note that the car tyres are often flat because there is hardly any pressure for various reasons including punctures. When the punctures are repaired and pressure is added using a pump, the car is able to go through most roads irrespective of their condition.

I find this example of a car with flat tyres to be the best analogy to explain part of our human condition. There are times we lead our lives like cars with flat tyres. We live as if there is no pressure within us. We drive through life like cars with flat tyres. We go through life with neither hope for the future nor excitement about the life we are living. Have you ever reflected on what happens when the pressure in the car tyres is increased to the required standard? What about when you increase the pressure inside of you? Let me tell you what I discovered. When the pressure inside of me is stronger than the pressure outside of me, I am able to endure any situation or circumstance. I am motivated to keep moving and reach my final destination. So, when you increase the pressure inside you, you are able to get what you want in life. I call this pressure within you and me 'purpose'.

It is purpose that pushes us from inside and keeps us in motion. Our purpose is the pressure that keeps us going and makes us say 'Yes' to life. Our purpose is our 'Why' that gives meaning to our lives. This purpose is the foundation for our life that without it, our life would mean nothing. Our purpose is our vision for being in this universe. One of my favourite books says, 'Where there is no vision, the people perish'. This implies, if we have no pressure, no purpose, no why, no vision, we have nothing to keep us in motion. We are like cars with flat tyres that will eventually stop when the tyres are worn out and the engines stop.

Now take time to reflect on these questions. What is the purpose of your life? Why are you in this world? What is your personal mission in this universe? How will future generations know that your life was worth living? What is the vision for your life? What inspires you to get into action, be in action and to stay in action? Do you ever feel the pressure within you?

You probably know that there is a difference between you and a tree growing out in the forest. Though the tree might not know its purpose, it has its uses: wood, charcoal, paper, medicine and others. If a non-thinking creature like a tree can have a purpose, why not you – an uncommon creature endowed with miracle power and greatness? Take time to reflect on your purpose, on your vision and on your why. Journey to the core of your being and discover your personal mission.

When we compare our lives to a house, it is not very important to have a house but it is necessary to know why you have a house. What is the purpose of your house? Why are you continuing to pay the rent or mortgage on it? If you have a house and no one lives in it, it is useless and with time, it is likely to fall into ruin or be taken over by squatters. So is your life and my life. I am reminded of a classmate I met 10 years ago in Uganda. From the way he dressed, looked, and spoke, it was difficult for me to believe that he was the person I had studied with. His lips had been taken over by alcohol, his skin by wounds, and toes squatted by jiggers. As I talked to him, I kept thinking that if he had applied what we learnt on vocation, his life would be different.

Likewise, if we are not using our life for its purpose, it can easily be taken over by squatters such as alcohol, drugs, excessive eating and all sorts of self-distracting behaviours. A squatted house is not useful to you, neither is a squatted body. So, taking time to discover your purpose and feel the pressure within you will help you get rid of all the squatters in your life. I believe that until one finds their purpose, life isn't worth living for 'the purpose of life is to live a life of purpose' (Robin Sharma).

A life tribunal?

The sad news is that most people never discover their purpose. They wake up because they have to, sleep because they have to, and eat because they have to. They walk through life without any purpose or vision for their lives. The famous author George Bernard Shaw suggests that we should establish a tribunal where at the end of each year, we go to defend ourselves on why we should be allowed to live another year. The great writer Mark Twain would add, 'The two most important days in your life are the day you are born and the day you find out why'. Effectively, the day you and I win our cases in this life tribunal will be a great day.

The great news is that you do not have to wait for the life tribunal. You have the power to win your tribunal case today. The starting point is to find your purpose: it is your compass through life. Search for your purpose, it is your Satnav through the interlocking streets of life. Though most people use a Satnav when they are driving from A to B, they rarely have a Satnav for their own life! They do not see where their life is going. This is a dangerous way of living. Like driving aimlessly without a Satnav is dangerous, so is living without purpose or a vision. An African proverb says, 'If you don't stand for something, you will fall for anything'. I would not wish this to happen to you. If I were you, I would decide to have a vision for my life today. Take time and discover the vision for your life. Let this vision be the ground of your being. Allow your vision to become your magnificent obsession.

People who have found their purpose are uncommon. They live, see, and act differently. You will experience this when you find your purpose. Like them, your heart will pump with purpose and not blood. Your eyes will not see random events but visions of a better future for you, for your family and for the rest of the universe. Your ears will hear not the noises of distractions but the calling to greatness. You will allow your feet not to walk anywhere but to where your treasure is hidden. You will walk with purpose. You will eat with purpose. You will sleep with purpose. You will talk with purpose. You will hear with purpose. You will see with purpose. What a transformed human being you will become after discovering your purpose. What a great life you will aim for once you have found your why for living.

I am a pencil

Let me share with you how I discovered my purpose. It is my hope that, if you are yet to discover your purpose, my experience will give you a clue to discovering yours. The clue to my purpose was in the name my parents gave me. I was born in Tooro Kingdom in Western Uganda, Africa. The language spoken in Tooro Kingdom is Rutooro and most of the people who live there are called Batooro. It is custom among the Batooro to give unique names to their children. Unlike in Europe, they do not have family names, this is based on the belief that each person is unique. Given that I was born in Tooro, my parents named me 'Businge'. When my name 'Businge' is translated in English, the equivalent word is 'peace'. I was born at a time when my parents were experiencing peace.

When I look back and connect the dots, I realise that whatever I have been doing with my life is in alignment with my name: 'Businge'. I therefore believe my purpose in life is to be a pencil in the hand of God and write three chapters with my life: be an instrument of peace, a messenger of hope and a channel of greatness. I believe that purpose leaves clues. As you continue to read this book, I recommend that you follow all the clues that may lead you to discover your purpose if you haven't found it yet. As it is for me, your purpose might be hidden in your name, in the place you were born, in the circumstances that led to your existence and even in the career you are currently pursuing. You may as well be inspired by reading about the lives of great men and women to help you find your purpose. Should you need further assistance in discovering your purpose, Greatness University will be there to help.

Deepen your belief

Before moving on to the next point, let me share with you one of the deepest secrets. I wouldn't share this with you had I not experienced it myself. Here is the secret: your level of belief is directly proportional to what you can make happen. The more you believe, the more you will actualise and vice versa. You must, then, believe in your vision and know it is possible. I would like you to start by saying to yourself: 'It is possible to live my vision'. May this affirmation be the fuel for your life. From today onwards, resolve to find your purpose and don't stop searching until you find it. Once you have found it, resolve to align your life with your purpose.

My life could have been different had I not found my purpose: being an instrument of peace in the world, messenger of hope in people's hearts and a channel of greatness in the world. This is why I wake up every morning. This is my vision. This is my calling. This is my personal mission. This is the reason I will give to the tribunal to defend my case for staying alive next year. I want life to use me and to make my vision possible. All I am and all I ought to be is focused on building this vision. Like St Teresa of Calcutta, Nelson Mandela, Mahatma Ghandi, Martin Luther Jr, and Jesus Christ, my vision is something I am willing to live for and die empty. I urge you to find your vision and get attached to it. Let it become your daily obsession.

A large vision

I have shared with you my vision not to impress but to impress upon you. As you might have noticed, your vision needs to be magnetic so that it can always attract you and align the inverse towards its realisation. Your vision needs to attract people, circumstances and resources onto your side that will make it possible. Your vision also needs to be compelling so that it repels the storms and hurricanes that you are likely to face in your life.

Remember what the motivation speaker Robert Schuller gave as a title to his book: *Tough Times Never Last, Tough People Do*. I trust that you are not going to give up on your vision. Remember, your vision needs to be grandeur, something bigger than yourself. Having a larger vision will give you room to grow into it. Given that your vision is very big, it is impossible to attach a monetary value to it. If you follow your vision just for the money, you will end giving up when you do not see the returns. In other words, follow Steve Jobs and 'Do what you love and love what you do… If you love what you do, you will never work a day in your life'.

As you continue to read this book, I would like you to develop a deep hunger for your vision and have an unquenchable thirst to actualise it. As you collect the materials to build your vision, I would like you to move with urgency and act in uncommon ways. As you build your vision, I would like you to live from a place of hope and not despair. From today onwards, I would like you to know that discovering your vision is a milestone to stepping into your greatness.

Your vision is calling you to dance to its music. The author Helen Keller says, 'The only thing worse than being blind is having sight but no vision'. Like Helen Keller, the worst thing you can do is to listen to your vision calling you and fail dance to its music. If you cannot dance according to your vision, get someone else to help you learn how to dance. If you cannot see your vision, ask other people who have seen their visions to help you. Do not go to people who may have a limited vision of themselves. If they do, how can they have a larger vision for you? Get a good mentor to help you see your vision. This could be someone you love, like or trust.

If you were to be asked at the end of our life's journey: What was the purpose of your life? What did you really want from the life you have just lived? Your response should resonate with that of Robin Sharma in his book *The Monk Who Sold His Ferrari* that 'The purpose of life is to live a life of purpose'. Find your purpose and allow it be the sole reason for you waking up every morning. Let it be the reason you stay standing. Let your vision be your personal mission, your why, and your purpose in this life. Allow your vision to show you your destination. Allow your vision to help you to see how you fit in this world so that you do not become a misfit. Allow your vision to propel you to your greatest life.

Final Reflection

As you come to the end of your second step to greatness, I hope you have discovered your purpose. I hope you have found what you desire most in this immense universe. If you have found it, guard it like the apple of your eye. Robert Collier says, 'Hold in your mind the thing you most desire. Affirm it. Believe it to be an existing fact…. You can have anything you want - if you want it badly enough… Your desire must be visualised, must be persisted in, must be concentrated upon, must be impressed upon… If you can visualise the thing you want, if you can impress upon your subconscious mind the belief that you have it, you can safely leave to it the finding of the means of getting it…' Take time and use the fire within you to find, reflect, visualise and act upon your purpose every minute and every hour of every day. You have something special. You have the pressure within you to move you to the next step to greatness.

---

*Before moving on to the next step, complete the activities for **STEP 2** in the accompanying workbook titled '7 Steps to Greatness: The Workbook to Take Your Life, Studies, Career and Business to the Next Level'.*

STEP 3: Dream While Awake

'Dream as if you'll live forever, live as if you'll die today'. James Dean

When I was young I used to have lots of dreams. I dreamt flying in the clouds like a bird and enjoying the view from above. I dreamt of running as lions chased me and suddenly waking up before they devoured me. I dreamt of sharing my favourite meal as I visited relatives and enjoyed being in their presence. I dreamt of the games I had played during the day and how I did not want them to come to an end. All these and many other dreams happened while I was asleep. Like me, you probably had similar dreams. These are only a small percentage of the dreams that took place while we were in our subconscious state as most of our dreams went unnoticed.

Nowadays, I have different dreams. More than ever, I am aware of all my dreams and most of them are becoming true. This has been possible because I have climbed the first two steps to greatness. While in the first step, I have taken time to know myself, I have discover my purpose in the second step. You too have taken the same steps and I can only imagine that you are already noticing the way you dream is changing. You should have started dreaming while you are awake because, unlike many people, you are uncommon and you possess the miracle power to do so.

This is what I am calling you to do in this third step to greatness: to have big dreams while you are fully conscious. You are going to take James Dean's advice and 'dream as if you'll live forever, live as if you'll die today'. You might be asking: what type of dreams are you talking about? What do dreams have to do with my purpose? In order to answer these questions, allow me share with you my story that I would have not told you had I not experienced it.

Live in war but don't let war live in you

We had just finished our dinner in the back courtyard under the light of the moon. Like every other night, we were getting ready to sleep. Suddenly there was noise and gunshots outside. With my parents and two elder brothers, we left our house by the back gate and ran into the banana plantations. That was the beginning of a long night that we spent in the banana plantations when rebels attacked our village. When we came back in the morning, part of our house was destroyed, my parents' shop had been burgled and my primary school had become an army barracks. I remember my family and many other people travelling in refugee truck being displaced to another county. That was the start of a life without schooling, of living in a new village with different people, and a time to dream while awake.

I was defined by this moment in Uganda as it brought me very close to my purpose. From this moment and thereafter, I was able to dream about the country I wanted to create and live in. I was called by something within me to use my life as an instrument of peace and a channel of hope beyond the war zone I was living in. In the midst of war and displacement, how was I to achieve my purpose? How was I to live my vision? For this to happen, allow me to share with you what I did and learnt from living in a war torn country, coming from a small village, poverty stricken and no one could have imagined any one of us escaping these adverse circumstances.

I had not only to let the moment define me but I had to define the moment too. Though I was living in war during those years, I did not let war live in me. The belief that war was not permanent allowed me to dream while I was awake.

During the one year while I was out of school, I dreamt of going back to school and completing my education. I dreamt of completing my education in a world class university. I dreamt of teaching about peace and writing stories that restored hope in people. The adverse circumstances I lived in allowed me to dream big. This was the best time in my life as a dreamer.

And after years of working on my dreaming, most of these dreams have come true. I have studied in over 7 universities and acquired approximately 10 post graduate degrees because I had a dream of education. I have been able to complete my Doctorate in Education at the University of Exeter now ranked 93rd in the Times Higher Education World University Rankings and one of the finest universities in the world. I have gone on to publish my first book titled, 'Education, Disability and Armed Conflict'. In educating myself, in writing and publishing my books, I have been able to shape how education could be used as an instrument of peace in countries that have or are experiencing war. I have been able to reach out to millions of people who read my books and have the potential to make a difference in their communities. In this example, my intention is not to show off but to allow you to see how my earliest dreams and circumstances have aligned with my purpose - being an instrument of peace in the world.

Dream big and save the world

I have shared with you my earliest dreams to impress upon you that if you follow your dreams, they will become true. If you are still searching for your dreams, look at your earlier years. Like it was for me, there may be seeds that you can plant and grow your wildest dreams. Like me, you might be inspired to become an instrument of peace. Remember, now more than ever, we need peace in a world torn by war, hatred and religion. There is great need for peace in our hearts, peace in our homes, peace in our countries and peace that lasts.

War starts inside of us. If we can calm the war within us, there would be no war outside of us. As we embark on the mission of being instruments of peace, we need follow St Francis of Assisi and ask, 'Where there is hatred, let me sow love; where there is injury, pardon; where there is doubt, faith; where there is despair, hope; where there is darkness, light; where there is sadness, joy'.

I encourage you to have a larger vision and dream big. If you have a limited vision for your life, your dreams will also be small. When you have a large vision and storms come your way, your larger vision will defend you and your dreams. In return, your big dreams will shelter you and your larger vision against the storms of life. In his acclaimed book *As a Man Thinketh*, James Allen writes, 'The dreamers are the saviours of the world'. You can only be a saviour of the world when you have big dreams. It is possible for you to have big dreams. So, decide to dream big today and be a great dreamer. Decide to be a saviour of the world by acting on your big dreams.

I used to believe that people who were very successful were lucky until I came across George Bernard Shaw's quote that 'People are always blaming their circumstances for what they are. I don't believe in circumstances. The people who get on in this world are the people who get up and look for the circumstances they want, and if they can't find them, make them.' This message allowed me to make a transition as I stopped believing that the current dreamers achieved their dreams overnight.

I stopped believing that dreamers who are successful, were and are lucky. I discovered that they dream big and take massive action. That they fight for their dreams through the storms of life. That they go beyond their circumstances and make things happen. Like Socrates, they believe that 'no human condition is ever permanent'. Like the co-founder of the Microsoft Corporation Bill Gates, they recognise that, 'If you are born poor it is not your problem. But if you die poor, it is your problem'. This is the attitude I wish you to have as you dream big and become a saviour of the world.

Sacrifice freedom for big dreams

Though I was born in a very poor family in Uganda, I had big dreams. Dreaming big was one of the treasures that my siblings and I had while growing up. We inherited dreaming big from our parents who too had big dreams. Our parents believed education was our only ticket out of poverty and as a result, worked day and night to make their dreams become true. Though they still struggled to get fees so that my siblings and I received a good education, they did not let their struggles become their benchmark.

I vividly remember when my father got into debt due to paying our school fees. One of the people whom he had borrowed money from took legal action and he was imprisoned. After two weeks in a prison cell, one of our family friends gave money to him so that he could use it to buy his freedom from prison. But as it was the start of the new school term and I had to go to school, he chose to stay in prison so that I could have the money to pay off my school fees. My father stayed in prison for his dream. He sacrificed his freedom so that I received education. What an uncommon person he was. Allow me to ask you one question: Which dream are you prepared to sacrifice everything for? If you can find one, then you are already a big dreamer.

Though we were materially poor, we did not let poverty live in us. We were rich because we had big dreams. Like my parents, I believed that it was possible to achieve my dreams. Like my parents, I decided that education was my only road out of poverty. From an early age, I decided to get the highest form of education so that I became a symbol of education greatness in my family. Since I had received the gift of education and knowing that my life was a gift and how I lived it was my gift, my dream was to give the gift of education to my siblings and to those who crossed my path.

As a result, my school holidays were not spent watching TV or playing computer games that never existed in our village. I spent my holidays working at my local church so that I could get money to pay part of my education. In the hot sunshine of Uganda, I mowed the church compound and worked on the church farm. There were times when I was asked to teach my local language to the American missionaries who came to visit our church. Like my parents, no matter how hard it was or worse it got, I did not lose sight of my big dream. My question to you is: are you prepared to never lose sight of your dreams? What will keep you focused on your dreams?

Step out of the frame and change your life

I have heard it said that 'you cannot see the picture when you are in the frame'. Leaving my parents' home allowed me to see the picture since I spent most of my time in a boarding school. The differences between my home environment and school were very noticeable. Here was the picture I saw and you can put the frame on it. My school had buildings built out of bricks. My parents' house was made from poles and mud. My school had electricity, my home relied on the moon and stars for light. I remember spending nights at my school reading in the school library. I also vividly remember how I spent my holidays at home, seated under the moon and the stars revising for my exams. At school, I had running water for my shower. At home before having a shower, I had to walk for approximately 30 minutes to draw water from the well and then use it to bathe.

I am glad that I stepped out of the frame and looked at my home picture from afar. Among the Batooro people of Western Uganda we have a saying, 'a child who does not travel thinks their mother is the best cook in the world'. Had I not stepped out of the frame and travelled to other destinations, I would still be in the same frame at home. Travelling allowed me to widen my frame and enlarge my dreams further. Before we move on, allow me to ask a couple of questions. Are you willing to widen your frame? Are you curious enough to explore what is beyond your current circumstances?

Live in poverty but don't let poverty live in you

In the summer of 1998, I came back from my missionary studies in Arusha, Tanzania. This was after one year of not being at home and one year of being outside the frame. I found my mother, two brothers and two sisters at home. My father was not at home as he was working for very little money in the tea factory. On that evening, we were seated in the living room and it was raining. Normally when it rained at the missionary school in Arusha, Tanzania it would only rain outside. But on the day I came home, it was raining both outside and inside our house!

One of my sisters ran to the bedroom to collect a bucket to catch the water that was coming through the roof. As she did this, a strong wind came and brought in more rain through one side of our house. Then my young brother ran to the bedroom to make sure water was not going through the walls to the mattress I was to sleep on. As night came, the main door lock was broken and my brother had to ensure the door was shut using a piece of wood.

In life, there are moments that either define you or you define them. This moment both defined me and I defined it. Switching from school to home and vice versa made me realise that our condition at home was not permanent. This was the moment when I realised that I was living in poverty but poverty was not living in me. I invite you to say with me: 'I have had it'. On this day, I said to myself: 'I have had it'. From this day, I decided to never allow poverty to live in me. On this day, I decided to have a plan of action to fight for my dream. From this moment, I set myself a goal: to build a family home that was better than the dormitory I slept in while I was at school. This dream became possible 10 years later. For people with big dreams, time is not important. What is essential is keeping focused on the dream.

Crave for your dreams

Sorry I have taken a lot of your time talking about my dreams. My intention is to show you how I have lived my dreams against the odds. My intention is to help you realise that when you dream big, obstacles become insignificant. Take time to reflect about your situation now since you may be having your own challenges that are similar or greater than mine. Despite these challenges, what are you willing to hang onto in your life? Circumstances may be going against you but remember Socrates is saying to you now, 'no human condition is ever permanent'.

I would like you to imagine all your challenges gone and imagine living your wildest dream now. Use these affirmations to strengthen your belief in your dreams so that no person or circumstance steals them from you:

- It is possible I can live my dream.

- I must work on my dream every day.

- It is not over until I achieve my dream.

- I will fight for my dreams until I win.

- No matter how hard it is or bad it gets, I will walk to my dream with a spirit of optimism.

It took me over 20 years to achieve my dream of getting a PhD in Education: the highest form of education I desired. I can say that my life would have been different had my parents not held onto their dream of education. However, too many people give up and don't fight for their dreams like you and me. They get scared and stop craving for their dreams when they face obstacles. As Les Brown says, 'Too many of us are not living our dream because we are living our fears'.

The choice is yours to make. Do you want to live your dreams or live your fears? Are your past failures hindering you to fight for your dreams? Les Brown says, 'There comes a time when you have to drop your burdens in order to fight for yourself and your dreams'. The time is now. Wanting your dreams is not enough. Having dreams is not enough. Being hungry for your dreams is not enough. You must crave for your dreams. Use the fire burning inside of you and refuse to fall behind in your dreams. Use the pressure within you to climb the steps to your greatness.

If you are not yet feeling the fire inside you, then, you have not yet got big dreams. If you have not yet discovered your dreams, keep searching. As you search for your dreams, your dreams are seeking you too. Refuse to stand on the corner of the street and park yourself and your dreams. This is the worst thing you can do to your dreams: park them. Give your dreams a chance to cruise on the motorway of life.

Can you imagine looking back on your life only to discover you have not lived your dreams? Can you imagine reaching at the end of your life only to discover you are dying with your dreams? The American author Henry David Thoreau best captures the regret thus, 'Oh, God, to reach a point of death only to realise that you have never lived'. It is a frightening thought, isn't it? Imagine your dreams coming to you and lamenting, 'we came to you so that you would give us life but you parked us on the motorway, taking away our life, when only you could have given us life'. If you are seeking to live your dreams, use your time on this planet to find them. Use your time to live your dreams not your fears.

Keep moving forward

Probably you know the message I am about to give. As you journey to your dreams, you will get tired and exhausted. You will lose enthusiasm. You will struggle to see and follow the road to your dreams. When this happens, your life 'Satnav' will fail you. The pressure within you will decrease. The fire within you will seem to extinguish. In these moments, you will stop and park your dreams.

When this happens, my advice to you is to never stop fighting for your dreams. Let nobody, no event or circumstance steal your dreams from you. In these moments, Martin Luther Jr who struggled as he fought for his dream of civil rights in America advises you thus: 'If you can't fly, then run, if you can't run, then walk, if you can't walk then crawl, but whatever you do you have to keep moving forward'. Like Martin Luther Jr, the courage that has brought you this far in this book and has allowed you to climb the third step should help you to keep moving.

If I were you, I would strengthen what is left and crawl through the streets of life with my dreams on my back as I search for the way to my greatness. If I were you, during this moment when the streets seem dark and I cannot see the path, I would still raise my feet hoping the path will appear. In these moments when I would feel like a car with tyres that have run out of pressure or with my legs that have run out energy to keep going, I would open my MUG and drink the greatness that is in it. This would give me the miracle power to stay in action, the determination to remain uncommon and the gift to be unstoppable in the pursuit of my greatest gift.

Final Reflection

You have come to the end of the THIRD STEP to greatness. You have had the chance to dream big while you are awake. I hope you have discovered your wildest dreams. Take time, use the fire within you and work on your dreams every minute, every hour of every day. Before we move on to the next step, here is my most important advice to you. Do not let fear become your standard. Allow life to use you to live your dreams and not your fears. Let your daily affirmation be: 'I want life to use me'. Increase the faith in your heart of your hearts that all your dreams are possible. Take action and 'Go after your dream with a sense of entitlement…Be willing to get up in life's face, grab it by the collar and say: "Give it UP! It's my dream' (Les Brown). If your dream is hard, do it harder. Tell yourself each day: 'I deserve my dreams'. I believe in you. I believe in your dreams. Live your dreams not your fears.

> *Before moving on to the next step, complete the activities for STEP 3 in the accompanying workbook titled '7 Steps to Greatness: The Workbook to Take Your Life, Studies, Career and Business to the Next Level'.*

7 Steps to Greatness

STEP 4: Develop STAR Goals

'The tragedy of life doesn't lie in not reaching your goal. The tragedy lies in having no goal to reach'.
Benjamin E Mays

What amazing success you have had since you started stepping into your greatness. You now know who you are. You know the purpose for your life. You have a lot of big dreams you want to accomplish. You have now reached the point of no return on your journey to greatness. As you step onto this fourth step, you cannot afford to go back to who you were before with your unclear vision and fuzzy dreams. The time and energy you have invested in your journey up to this point is greater than what you will need to reach your destination. Like an athlete, you can only focus on reaching the finishing line and winning the race.

On the finishing line is clearly marked LIVE YOUR DREAMS. You have clear images of the great life you will live once you reach the finishing line. Now is the time for you to bridge the gap between what you have in your mind and want you want to manifest in reality. It is time for you to choose a route that is going to take you to your dreams and design a plan of action. In this step, I will introduce you to S.T.A.R© goals: the best route to your wildest dreams.

Big dreams need big goals

To be able to reach the big dreams you have, you need big goals. Goals are the reasons your dreams will stand or fall. Goals are the pillars to your dreams. Goals are the fuel to your dreams. People who live without goals muddle and wander through life without knowing where they are going. They sleep walk through life. Goals will help you move from where you are to where you want to go. I was lucky to listen to Les Brown and realise that 'many people fail in life not because they aim too high and miss. Many people fail because they aim too low and hit'. This made me question how big and high my goals were.

Let us take time and compare goals to pillars in the house. If you are looking for pillars to build a house that will last, you need strong pillars. There are different types of pillars in the marketplace. The type of pillars you buy and use will determine how strong your house is going to last. Just as you would go for the best pillars to support your house, go for the best goals that will propel you to your dreams. While looking for goals, I found the best ones at the Les Brown Institute in Fort Lauderdale, Florida. They are called **S.T.A.R**© goals. These have become the highway to my dreams. The acronym **S.T.A.R**© stands for:

- Strongly felt by you and connected to your dreams;

- Theatre of your mind;

- Absolutely necessary;

- Ridiculously hard to achieve.

Let us now take time and examine what each of these pillars represents and how they may help you achieve your dreams.

Strongly felt and connected

One of my favourite books says, 'For where your treasure is, there your heart will be also'. Your dreams are your treasures. Your goals need to go and be attached to your treasures in your heart. Your goals need to go and make the heart their domicile. If your goals are not strongly connected to your dreams in your heart, you will experience difficulties in achieving them. When difficulties come, you will give up because your heart is not connected to your goals and vice versa. Your goals must be everything to you. You must be willing to do whatever it takes to achieve them. You must be ready to move heaven and earth in order to achieve them.

Allow me to share with you one of my goals. I would not share this with you if I did not trust you. Early this year, I was experiencing severe pain attacks on one side of my head. Whenever they would come, they would last for at least 30 minutes. When I went to my doctor, he diagnosed neuralgia and gave me a prescription signing me off from work for three months. After taking the medication for one week, there was no change to my painful condition. When I went back to my doctor, he increased the dosage.

Knowing that my health was my wealth, my goal was to recover form neuralgia no matter what it costed me. This belief led me to search and use alternative treatments, one of them being osteopathy. After two sessions at the osteopathy clinic, there was still no change and during that time, I came to realise that the pain was coming from a localised part of my head. So, I made an appointment with my dentist. During this appointment, the dentist discovered I had an infected tooth which was causing me severe pain. I went back the next day and had the tooth removed. The pain stopped.

During this time of severe pain, my goal was to recover my health without which I could not achieve my dreams. You would not be reading this book now had I not achieved my goal of having a healthy and pain-free life. I believe that I achieved this goal because it was strongly connected to my heart. Let me tell you how. I searched for various forms of treatment and visited several medical practitioners until I got the one that worked for me. If my goal was not connected to my heart and to my dreams, I would have decided to just sit at home, sleep, continue being off work, get sick pay and possibly die with my pain.

My advice to you is that you must have goals that enable you to live your dreams not your fears. You have to want your goals badly enough that without them you cannot achieve your dreams. If your goals are strongly felt and connected to your dreams, you will be excited and on fire to achieve them. Your goals will fuel your dreams and increase your motivation. You will wake up passionate about attaining them. If your goals are connected to your heart, you will feel them in your heart of hearts and the pressure within you will push you towards their accomplishment.

In the theatre of your mind

Not only should your goals be strongly felt in your heart, they also need to be played out in the theatre of your mind. Before you can attain your goals, you must be able to visualise them vividly on the screen of your mind. You must be able to see them with clarity and how their successful completion will transform your life. I imagine Steve Jobs visualised the iPhone and other Apple products on the screen of his mind before producing them as physical products that have now transformed the lives of billions of people all over the world.

It is only when we see our goals on the screen of our minds that we believe they are possible. I therefore encourage you to picture your goals in your mind every day. Close your eyes and see your future self, future day to day activities, future business, future foundations, future bank accounts, future life and future personal economy. Let your mind become the theatre where the videos of your goals are played. Your videos could include being approved for a loan to complete your education; paying off your mortgage so that you can own your home; travelling the world in a cruise so that you can enjoy your retirement; starting a business so that you are financially free; writing your book so that you become a bestselling author.

Carry these animated videos in your mind and refer to them constantly during your day. Les Brown says, 'When you bring the future into the present with an incredibly vivid picture of your goal, your brain takes ownership of it; it wants it right there, right now'. Effectively, you have to see your goals as accomplished in your mind first before they are achieved in reality. Visualise how you would feel when you have accomplished them. Once this has happened in your mind, go into the world and start achieving them.

Absolutely necessary

You now know that your goals need to be felt in your heart and visible on the screen of your mind. The third feature of your S.T.A.R© goals is that they are absolutely necessary. This means your goals are a life-and-death issue to you. That was what my father did when he chose to stay in prison and give me the money which was to buy his freedom so that I can use it to pay school fees. For my father, my freedom from ignorance was greater than his freedom from prison. This was a life and death issue to him. From this experience, I learnt that if I was ever to achieve my dreams, I needed to make my goals absolutely necessary.

Allow me to share with you how this happened in my life in 2013. I was working as a fulltime teacher in the UK. My wife was not in fulltime employment. She was taking care of our daughter and expecting our youngest son in the same year. We were living in a one bedroom apartment that I had mortgaged at the height of the property boom in 2007 in the United Kingdom. As our family expanded, our dream was to move into a four bedroom house before the birth of our son in the same year.

As days passed by and the time for the birth of our son neared, the dream of moving homes became absolutely necessary for us otherwise we would end up sleeping four people in just one bedroom. We had to set ourselves goals. Our first goal was to call in a local estate agent to give us a valuation of how much our apartment was worth. The estate agent valued it lesser than I had bought it due to the economic depression. This was a setback to our dream!

During that time, my wife liked listening to Bishop T.D Jakes. As she had heard from him that 'a setback is a setup for a comeback', she decided to make a dream board. She put our dream house on the dream board and it became her daily obsession and goal to look at it and pray about it. My daily ritual was to search on property websites for our dream home. Our evening commitment after work was to make new mortgage applications until we got a yes. Our weekend habit was to view new homes within 50 miles from where we lived with the hope that we part-exchanged our apartment. After almost nine months of setting and resetting goals that were absolutely necessary to our dream, we achieved our dream.

When I reflect on this experience, this is what I learnt from this process and I wish to share with you now. Big dreams need big goals. For our goals to be realised, they need to be visible in our mind, felt in our hearts and absolutely necessary for us. Our quest to have a house before we got our second child became a daily obsession. As we did not want four of us to be crammed into a one bedroom apartment, getting a four bedroom house became a life and death issue to us. We were filled with an urgency to realise our goal or else it was not going to happen easily. We used our imagination to make our future dream house appear much more desirable than the present apartment we were living in. This created the urgency and momentum to go after our dream house in an unstoppable way.

On a deeper level, I now realise that there were other universal laws that were working on the background beyond our determination. One of them is that stated by the 13th century poet Rumi that 'what you seek is seeking you'. As we searched for our dream house, there were people, circumstances and time that were put in place so that we get what we wanted. Likewise, as you move towards your dreams, make your goals absolutely necessary that if they are not achieved, then your life will cease to continue. Once the universe notices your determination, it will give you support and answers so that you achieve your goals.

Ridiculously hard to achieve

This is the last feature of S.T.A.R© goals. Make your goals hard to achieve. This is probably what Dr Norman Vincent Peale meant by saying, 'Shoot for the moon and even if you miss, you'll land among the stars'. This is probably what Les Brown means when he says, 'Most people fail in life not because they aim too high and miss, but because they aim too low and hit'. If your goals are too easy, then you might end up failing. If your goals are too hard, even if you miss, you will have learnt from the process. The process of striving to achieve your goals is more important than achieving them. So, shoot for the moon. Have tough goals that will keep you inspired and focused rather than shoot for the stars because you may hit and fail.

As you already know, my current vision is to be an instrument of peace in the world, a messenger of hope in people's hearts and a channel of greatness in the world. My dream is to get at least one million people to share this tripartite vision with me so that they too become instruments of peace, messengers of hope and channels of greatness. I have set myself three ridiculously hard to achieve goals: to write and help people write books on peace, hope and greatness; make Greatness University a world leader in the study on greatness; and inspire hope in the people I meet.

These are hard goals to achieve. They are all set outside my comfort zone because great things happen outside our comfort zones. Like me, take time to think about your goals in the various areas of your life - what are your relationship goals? Financial goals? Spiritual goals? Education goals? Health goals? How easy or hard are they to achieve? For your goals to be ridiculously hard to achieve, you need to set them outside your comfort zone but not too far that it becomes impossible to achieve. Even if you do not achieve your goals, it is worth going through the process. Most people focus on the end goal, missing the process. In S.T.A.R goals, the process is more valuable than the outcome.

Final Reflection

You now know how S.T.A.R© goals can help you reach your dreams. As you journey, use goals that you feel in your heart and are visible on the screen of your mind. As you shoot for your dreams, have goals that are a life and death issue to you and stretch you to the limits of your existence. As you build your dreams, have goals that are strong enough to support them and push you towards the stars. As you journey to your dreams, have goals that will drive you to a higher purpose. As you crave for your dreams, have a mentor to help you lock your goals into your heart and write them on the screen of your mind. This way, you will live your dreams and not your fears. This way, you will step into your greatness and not forever stay in your comfort zone.

> *Before moving on to the next step, complete the activities for* **STEP 4** *in the accompanying workbook titled '7 Steps to Greatness: The Workbook to Take Your Life, Studies, Career and Business to the Next Level'.*

STEP 5: See With Vision

'The only thing worse than being blind is having sight but no vision'. Helen Keller

By now you know what you want from life. You want to make your vision a reality. You want to live your dreams and achieve your STAR goals. For this to happen in reality, you need to clearly see it in your mind first. Napoleon Hill says, 'Whatever the mind of man can conceive and believe, it can achieve'. This means the ability to see what you want from life is essential to getting what you want. This is called visualisation: a method for programming your mind to see with clarity your vision, your dreams and your goals. In this fifth step, I will give you the **V.I.S.I.O.N©** system to help you see what you want from life. The acronym **V.I.S.I.O.N©** stands for:

- Visualise

- Inside the mind

- Senses

- Imagine

- Overcome obstacles

- No fear

To help you remember this **V.I.S.I.O.N©**, I urge you to learn this sentence: I Visualise Inside my mind with my Senses and I Imagine Overcoming obstacles with No fear. Let us now explore each feature of this **V.I.S.I.O.N©**.

Visualise

In her book *Creative Visualisation*, Shakti Gawain indicates that visualisation 'involves understanding the natural principles that govern the workings of our universe, and learning to use these principles in the most conscious and creative ways'. Visualisation gives us the power to make things, events and circumstances real in our minds. We can visualise what we want in any domain of our life: cooking, sports, prayer, marriage, education, business, and many others.

Research shows that successful men and women use visualisation to win in various domains. For example, the business expert and entrepreneur Grant Cardone says that visualisation makes his goals become real. On his blog he writes, 'When I was first starting my business, I wrote down my goals every day. I cut out pictures of where I wanted to live and looked at those pictures every day. The reason I did this was because it reminded me every single minute what I was working for. It reminded me that if I went home at the end of my work day that I still had more work to do if I wanted to achieve my success'. Visualisation is not only used by business people but also by sports men and women. For example, athletes visualise themselves winning the race before they even run the race. Footballers visualise themselves winning the match before they play it. This means the race or the match is first won in the mind before it is worn in reality. This implies winning the race or playing the match in reality is only a formality.

To visualise effectively, you need to decide what you want to visualise. Once you have decided what you want to visualise, create a mental picture and focus on it as many times as possible. For example, if you want to perform to the very best at work, visualise your best day at work before you leave your home. Before waking up or as you take your shower, take time to watch the great day you are going to have unfold on the screen of your mind. See yourself arriving at your workplace. Notice the surroundings: the people, buildings, plants, smells, sounds, etc. Call to mind the tasks you have to perform. If there are many tasks, rank them in the order of importance. Envision yourself doing each task starting with the most important with total concentration. Tell yourself that you will block out all the distractions happening around you. As you perform each task, feel confident, cheerful and focused. Perform each task on your list from start to finish in your mind before beginning a new task. Visualise your supervisor appreciating the way you did your work. See yourself leaving the workplace at the end of the day happy and proud of what you have achieved.

Inside the mind

This is the second aspect of V.I.S.I.O.N©. It is in the mind where visualisation takes place. Robert Collier says, 'We can do only what we think we can do. We can be only what we think we can be. We can have only what we think we can have. What we do, what we are, what we have, all depend upon what we think. We can never express anything that we do not first have in mind. The secret of all power, all success, all riches, is in first thinking powerful thoughts, successful thoughts, and thoughts of wealth, of supply. We must build them in our own mind first'.

This means whatever we achieve as human beings we create them first as an idea. Plato refers to this as the world of forms: a world where we find ideals of that which exists. So, an artist finds the idea of a portrait before painting it. A singer gets the idea of the song before singing it. An author gets the idea of a book before writing it. An inventor has the idea of an iPhone before making it. And you have the idea of your greatest life before you can live it. In truth, our ideas are blueprints that eventually become real outside our minds when we act upon them.

So, if you want to live your dreams and achieve your goals, visualise them first. You may find it helpful to write them down, create mental imageries, speak about them, and even have physical models. This is what great people do: they create in their minds what they want from life. Take time and notice how Martin Luther King Jr does this in this excerpt taken from his speech: *I Have Been to the Mountain Top* delivered in Memphis, Tennessee on 3rd April 1968.

And you know, if I were standing at the beginning of time, with the possibility of taking a kind of general and panoramic view of the whole of human history up to now, and the Almighty said to me, "Martin Luther King, which age would you like to live in?" I would take my mental flight by Egypt and I would watch God's children in their magnificent trek from the dark dungeons of Egypt through, or rather across the Red Sea, through the wilderness on toward the Promised Land. And in spite of its magnificence, I wouldn't stop there.

I would move on by Greece and take my mind to Mount Olympus. And I would see Plato, Aristotle, Socrates, Euripides and Aristophanes assembled around the Parthenon. And I would watch them around the Parthenon as they discussed the great and eternal issues of reality. But I wouldn't top there.

I would go on, even to the great heyday of the Roman Empire. And I would see developments around there, through various emperors and leaders. But I wouldn't stop there.

I would even come up to the day of the Renaissance, and get a quick picture of all that the Renaissance did for the cultural and aesthetic life of man. But I wouldn't stop there.

I would even go by the way that the man for whom I am named had his habitat. And I would watch Martin Luther as he tacked his ninety-five theses on the door at the church of Wittenberg. But I wouldn't stop there.

I would come on up even to 1863, and watch a vacillating President by the name of Abraham Lincoln finally come to the conclusion that he had to sign the Emancipation Proclamation. But I wouldn't stop there.

I would even come up to the early thirties, and see a man grappling with the problems of the bankruptcy of his nation. And come with an eloquent cry that we have nothing to fear but "fear itself". But I wouldn't stop there.

Strangely enough, I would turn to the Almighty, and say, "If you allow me to live just a few years in the second half of the 20th century, I will be happy."

What great imagination Martin Luther King had that allowed him to climb to the mountain top and see the 'Promised land'. Like Martin Luther King, you have the power to visualise and reach your 'Promised Land' where greatness awaits you. The secret to this is to make visualisation your daily ritual. If you are finding your path to visualisation blocked, here is the key.

Senses

Senses are the keys to your mind. They help you access your mind faster so that you can see, smell, touch, feel, and taste what you want. You are where you are today because of what you have seen, touched, smelt, tasted, and felt. If you change what you are using your senses to do, your results will change too. Let me give you an example. I used my senses to visualize this book writing it. I could see it being published on the set date. I could see many people reading it. I could hear their comments as they read it. I could see the emotional journey they took and the personal transformation they went through as they turned each page. I could smell what was being eaten or drunk as people paused to reflect and complete the activities in the workbook. I, therefore, saw the completion of this book and what would happen after I published it on the screen of my mind because my senses allowed me to do so.

Had I decided that I was no longer going to commit my time to writing this book, you would not be reading it today. My mentor Brian Tracy says, 'As you change your mental pictures on the inside, your world on the outside will begin to change to correspond to those pictures'. What are you seeing? Smelling? Touching? Hearing? What movies are you playing to yourself? If you change the movies playing on the screen of your mind today, your life will change too. In other words, change your thoughts change your life.

I am reminded of the time I was doing my teacher training. My tutor told me a story of a student who, whenever she came for her lessons, she visualised her best piece of work being displayed in the classroom. That piece of work was a Christmas Calendar. It was done so well that the teacher displayed it in the classroom during the lifetime of that student in the school. One of the things this student did whenever she came to that department for a lesson, she would look at her Christmas Calendar, touch it and then go. One day the teacher asked her, 'Why do you usually come to my class?' Her reply was, 'I come to visit my Christmas Calendar'.

This visualisation visit set the standard of success this student wished to have in her other lessons. Seeing, touching, smelling, feeling, tasting her past success became a ritual that allowed her to increase her success rate in other subjects. This student allowed her past success set the standard for her future success. This is a habit of great and successful people. The world's number one success coach Brian Tracy explains, 'Prior to every new experience, the successful person visualises previous success experiences that are similar to the upcoming event'. Are there past successes in your life you can use as a springboard to your future success? I once listened to a teacher who was retiring after thirty years of service. Her colleagues considered her to be a great teacher. In her leaving speech she said, 'I was a great teacher for only one year and I repeated it thirty times'. Can you find great moments in your life that you can use to create other great moments? Who are the people you can follow so that their success rubs off on you? Remember success and greatness leave clues.

Imagine

Many people live from their memory most of the time. They let their past determine their present and future. They allow what has happened to determine what will happen. Albert Einstein says, 'imagination is more important than facts'.

This is because without imagination, it is difficult to create a future. Do you remember what I said about ideas? Things exist as ideas first before they exist in reality. It is imagination which allows us to see ideas on the screens of our minds. It is only after imagining that we are able to go and create facts in our physical environment.

From an early age, I had the idea of becoming a missionary. I then became a missionary for 10 years. After that I had the idea of becoming a teacher. I have been a teacher for the past 10 years. I then got the idea of becoming an entrepreneur. I have been for the past 5 years. Now I have the idea of becoming an international speaker, bestselling author and greatness coach. As you can see from my personal experience, without having the ideas and imagining those ideas becoming real, I would not be who I am, where I am, and what I am doing today. Without living from imagination, I would be behind in my dreams and my goals.

In *Secret of the Ages*, James Allen writes, 'Let a man alter his thoughts, and he will be astonished at the rapid transformation it will effect in the material conditions of his life'. So, change your thoughts, change your life. What are your dominant thoughts right now? Is it a new job? Is it buying a new home? Is it improving your memory? If you imagine the reality you want to create, you have the miracle power to manifest it in reality.

Imagination requires you to enter into a reflective and a quiet state of mind. Once you are in this state, then everything is possible. You can imagine any of the things you have wished for in life. If it is a new car, imagine yourself in your new car. Add the details of colour, seats, steering wheels, and the sunroof. Make your car real in your mind. Imagine who is with you in your new car. Imagine the sound your car makes as you turn on the engine. Imagine driving through the streets of where you live and through the country roads. As you imagine all of this, experience the imagination as if it has already happened. Be filled with a profound and unwavering belief that it is possible for you to have your new car in reality. Imagine as many times as you wish during the day, weeks, months, and years until your imagination and dreams become reality.

Consider having a board where you have pictures of what you imagine: your vision, your dreams, and your goals. As you journey to your dreams and step into your greatness, it is necessary that you live from imagination and not from memory. While memory will take you back to the past and increase your fears; imagination will increase your hope and drive you to the future where your dreams are possible. This has been my experience on many occasions. When I was training to be a teacher, I imagined myself teaching every day for 4 years. When I wanted to be a Doctor of Education, I imagined myself graduating with a PhD every day for 5 years. Using my imagination on a daily basis gave me the power to be relentless and remain unstoppable as I fought for my dreams.

Overcome obstacles

On this penultimate feature of the V.I.S.O.N© system, I would like to remind you that as you focus on your vision, obstacles will surely come. People will disappoint you. Distractions will come and find you. Many unexpected things will happen on the way to your greatness. What will you do? The bestselling author of the *Secrets of the Millionaire Mind* T Harv Eker makes this observation: 'Rich people focus on opportunities. Poor people focus on obstacles'. I would say in moments of obstacles, people who are uncommon and are stepping into their greatness focus on opportunities and not obstacles. Having the ability to see opportunities in the perceived obstacles allows them to work towards getting what they want from life. This is what separates them from the common people. This is what distinguishes them as people who live their dreams from those who live their fears.

You will therefore need to take control of what you are visualising in a given situation and not let obstacles get on the way to your greatness. You have complete control of what you want from life and there is no one stopping you but you. Take a look at where you are in life right now. Whatever you have achieved or not achieved is a product of how you have dealt with the obstacles which have come on your way. As you move into the future, do not let obstacles get in the way to living your dreams. Do not allow obstacles to make you stumble as you walk on the path to your greatness.

No fear

Welcome to the final aspect of the V.I.S.I.O.N© system. You have now developed the skills to visualise in your mind and with your senses what you want from life. You have realized that you are likely to meet obstacles on the way to your dreams. Your approach is going to be searching for opportunities in every perceived obstacles. This will be your vitamin to continue walking in the path to your dreams.

In this final aspect, we are going to focus on fear. In one of my favourite books Job says, 'The thing which I greatly feared has come upon me'. There will be times when your visualisation will take you to your fears like Job. If you intensely visualise your problems, you will get fearful. You will be scared of what is in your mind. Do you remember the story I narrated from Les Brown about the man who was always afraid of a dog in his neighborhood? He would always ran whenever the dog barked until he developed the courage to face the dog. It is only at this point he realized that the dog had no teeth. It is only when we decide to face our fears that we realize, like Dr Martin Luther King, that we have nothing to fear but fear itself.

Some people see FEAR as an acronym for two actions: **F**orget **E**verything **A**nd **R**un and **F**ace **E**verything **A**nd **R**aise. Which action will you take when faced with fear? If I were you, I would Face Everything and Raise because I have learnt from Dr Martin Luther King that the worst thing to fear is fear itself. I would raise and take Dr Norman Vincent Peale's advice to throw my heart over the fence and let my body follow. This would require immense faith. In my favourite book, St Paul writes: 'Faith is being sure of what we hope for and certain of what we do not see'. This means we are sure of what we do not see as a result of our **F.A.I.TH**. In other words, we **Find Answers In The Heart**.

Life is full of examples of people who have lived by FAITH in extraordinary ways: Mother Teresa, Nelson Mandela, Martin Luther King, Dietrich Bonhoeffer, and many others. Life is also full of people who have lived by FAITH in ordinary ways: our parents, siblings, neighbours, etc. In my case, FAITH is one of the treasures I got from my parents when they walked to their dreams with great determination and unwavering hope. This taught me that I can achieve my dreams if I lived from a place of FAITH. As you continue to see your VISION, do it from a place of FAITH not FEAR. FAITH will take you to another hemisphere with a different time zone where your dreams are possible.

Final Reflection

As you live with no fear, remember to visualize your FAITH. Visualisation will give you what you desire most: good or bad, success or failure, courage or fear, worry or happiness, hope or despair. Remember what Brian Tracy says, 'Sometimes, if your emotion is intense enough and your visual image is clear enough, your goal will immediately come true'. This means the more frequent you feed your mind with what you want, the quicker it will become possible. Take time to examine your FAITH. As you do this, I would like to leave this question with you: How big is your FAITH? Your response might be like that of the apostles after listening to Jesus talking about the challenges ahead that caused them to tremble: 'Lord, increase our faith'. Your response could also be 'Increase my VISION and FAITH' as I head towards the penultimate step to my greatness.

Before moving on to the next step, complete the activities for **STEP 5** *in the accompanying workbook titled '7 Steps to Greatness: The Workbook to Take Your Life, Studies, Career and Business to the Next Level'.*

STEP 6: Network With Great People

'Align yourself with people that you can learn from, people who want more out of life, people who are stretching and searching and seeking some higher ground in life'. Les Brown

When it comes to the people we associate with, there is no shortage of sayings, proverbs and statements. One African proverb says, 'Birds of the same feather flock together'. Another goes, 'Show me your friends and I will show you who you are'. The President of the United States of America Donald Trump says, 'If you hang around with losers you become a loser'. Porter Gale titled her book, 'Your Network is Your Net Worth'. So I say to you, if you want be great, surround yourself with great P.E.O.P.L.E© because greatness leaves clues. You might be asking: How do I know who the great P.E.O.P.L.E© are? Here is my simple answer: Great people are P.E.O.P.L.E© who are:

- Purposeful

- Encouraging

- Opportunity experts

- Productive

- Live full

- Exemplary

If you want to be great, take time and apply this formula to the people that you associate with. It is my hope that by the end of this penultimate step, you would have found out who the great P.E.O.P.L.E© are in your life.

Are the people you associate with PURPOSEFUL?

Great people are full of purpose. They know who they are and why they came into this world. You will recognise them when you meet them. They walk with purpose, eat with purpose, drink with purpose, and smile with purpose. They are filled with purpose. Given that they are filled with purpose, their purpose will overflow onto you. Make it your purpose to find people of purpose and get acquainted with them. Ask them what their purpose is and what drives them. Ask them how they walk to their dreams, achieve their goals, and listen to their ideas. Observe their experience with purpose and make them your role models.

Associating with purposeful people is not only limited to meeting with them personally. Most of the purposeful people are freely available to talk to you in your local library or waiting for you on social media channels such as YouTube, Facebook and Instagram. Purposeful people are already speaking to you through their audiobooks, videos, and CDs. They are there in your community making a positive difference. Always remember that now, and more than ever, you can access a lot of great people without leaving the comfort of your home – and for free!

When I look back at my life and connect the dots, I realise I did not have many opportunities to meet great people like I do now. I seem to have had a few people in my life who were filled with purpose and transmitted purpose to me. The first ones were my parents who fuelled my dreams. I remember my father choosing to pay my school fees and be imprisoned rather than pay off his debt. This showed me that he sacrificed his freedom for his purpose and dream: educating all his children up to university. From this I realised that while my father inspired my head, my mother ignited my heart. We will forever be grateful to our purpose filled parents.

The other group of people I had growing up were the missionaries who ran my local church. I decided to hang around with them because, from an early age, I knew that if I wanted to live a purpose filled life, I needed to associate with purposeful people. That was why I attended their schools. This opened a windows of opportunity for me to do missionary work in over 10 countries in Africa and Europe. During this time, I had the opportunity to learn various languages including French, Arabic, and Swahili. I associated with people of different races, cultures and religions.

I can vividly recollect the memorable moments while I lived in various countries. Driving into a town in Northern Uganda, where the only clothing people had was Adam's suit. You can now imagine what I saw when it rained and men and women continued walking in the rain. Using sign language in my first week in Burkina Faso to buy chewing gum in a shop only to realise I was eating food seasoning before swallowing it. Going to a funeral in Burkina Faso expecting to find people mourning for the deceased person laying in a coffin only to find people joyously dancing around the deceased person who was seated on a special throne. Getting lost in Algeria while looking for a church only to end up in a mosque that used to be a church. Despite these unexpected encounters, the missionary experience taught me that the purpose of my life was to live a life of purpose and contribution wherever I went.

Knowing my purpose allowed me, in the terms of the bestselling author of *Rich Dad Poor Dad* Robert Kiyosaki, to FOCUS: 'Follow One Strategy Until Successful'. It is therefore necessary that you know your purpose and FOCUS. Let me briefly share with you what unfocused people do. They start and never finish. They give in to distractions and lack concentration. They dream while they are asleep and sleepwalk during the day. Focused people, however, are like a postage stamp that stays on one envelope until the letter reaches its destination. They are glued onto what they do until completion. In my opinion, FOCUS is the highway to your purpose. If you are not focused, you will end up being average. Do not let distractions derail you from this highway.

At this point, it is worth for you to visualise the types of people you associate with. Are they filled with purpose? Are they focused? Are they glued on to their purpose like postage stamps? Look at your friends, relatives, work colleagues and all your relationships. Reflect deeply and ask yourself: What is this relationship doing to me? Is it giving me life or taking life away from me? Is this relationship helping me to focus or to be distracted? Am I winning or losing from this relationship? As you reflect on these questions, remember that if you surround yourself with losers, you will be a loser. If you surround yourself with winners, you will be a winner.

For you to change, the people you network with must also change too. Think about the specific field you are interested in. If you want to be a nurse, hang out with nurses. If you want to be a teacher, hang out with teachers. If you want to be successful, hang out with successful people. If you want to be rich, hang out with rich people. Watch what they do, listen to what they listen to, eat what they eat, dress the way they dress, emulate their habits and copy their strategies to success. Take Les Brown's advice and 'align yourself with people that you can learn from, people who want more out of life, people who are stretching and searching and seeking some higher ground in life'. Surround yourself with people who will help you to become a purposeful person. Follow their footprints until you reach the best version of you.

Are the people you associate with ENCOURAGING?

Great people are always encouraging and supportive as you to do what is good. I am reminded of my favourite verse in the timeless poem by Mary Stevenson 'Footprints in The Sand'. The verse goes: 'You promised that if I followed you, you would walk with me always. But I have noticed that during the most trying periods of my life there have only been one set of footprints in the sand. Why, when I needed you most, you have not been there for me? He replied, "The times when you have seen only one set of footprints, is when I carried you'. As you strive to do what is good and step into your greatness, you will experience many difficulties and failures along the way. It is necessary that surround yourself with people who can carry you in times of trouble. Surround yourself with encouraging people who will lift you up when you fall. Surround yourself with people who you learn from because they are the message they need to bring to you. Surround yourself with people who will always see the path to your greatness before you see it for yourself.

My mentor Les Brown has always said, 'If you can't pick people up in your life, for God's sake do not let them bring you down'. When trouble comes, great people will be there to encourage you. Like Dr Martin Luther King Jr, they know that 'only when it is dark enough can you see the stars'. They know you have to go through the darkness to be able to see the light. This means they are encouraging and supportive in the moments of darkness. So find people who will go with you through the darkness of the night to see the light of the stars.

Encouraging people are also positive in their dealings with you. They nourish you. They help you grow. They empower you. They inspire you. They allow you to manifest your greatness. At this moment in time, you might not know who these encouraging people are. Some people who are close to you may not be encouraging as you would like them to be. Do not get upset that your close friends won't encourage you as you step into your greatness. Do not let their lack of encouragement slow down your pace to greatness. From my personal observation, most encouraging people tend to be strangers. They are the people who will empower you and share your vision. They are the people who will stretch you mentally, spiritually, personally, etc. Remember too, proximity is power, so, find and hang around with people who will encourage you. Indeed, your ability to associate with encouraging people can make the difference between living your dreams or dying with your fears.

Are the people you associate with OPPORTUNITY experts?

Let me start with a popular African folktale. Long time ago, some birds and animals lived in the sky. The dog and the hen lived there, too. One day, it was very cold. The birds asked the dog to go down to the earth and bring some fire to make the sky warm. The dog went to the earth and entered a courtyard near the house. The dog saw many bones, started eating them, and forgot all about the fire. The dog decided to live there. As the birds in the sky were getting colder, they sent the hen. The hen came to the same courtyard. It saw seeds, started eating them, and forgot about the fire. The hen decided to live here. The dog and hen did not return to the sky because of the better opportunities they found on earth.

Only for illustration purposes, imagine you are a dog or hen. You have been sent to this amazing earth on a special mission. The earth is your courtyard filled with abundant opportunities. What are you willing to do? Great people are hungry to seize opportunities like the dog and hen. You too need to be hungry like the dog and hen for opportunities to make your dreams come true. Observe and seize the opportunities that will help you achieve your goals. I remember going to view a block of flats where we wanted to expand our serviced apartments business. While I was in a meeting with the company director and knowing how much money I had to invest, I told her I only needed 5 apartments. She replied, 'You have a big company. We are offering you 20 apartments'. I replied, 'Thank you, I will take them'.

I took the advice I had learnt from my supportive business mentor who told me that when an opportunity presents itself, say yes and work on the how later. At the time, I did not know where I was going to get the money to pay rent for 20 apartments. The same night, I had a guest who was living with us and during dinner, she asked me, how my day was. I narrated to her my encounter with the company director. She was interested in our business model and decided to joint venture on this project. I had seized my moment and she seized hers! Both of us seized our moments and made our business dreams a reality. I am telling you this story not to impress you but to imprint upon you that when you seize the moment, you are one step closer to realising your dreams. So, find and associate with people who are seeking for opportunities to live their dreams.

Before we move on to next feature of P.E.O.P.L.E©, allow me ask you: Have you ever wondered why a similar circumstance can happen to two people and one will succeed while the other would fail? The difference is how that circumstance is perceived. While one person might see that circumstance as an obstacle, another might see it as an opportunity. In his book *Secret of the Ages*, Robert Collier writes, 'The successful man sees opportunity, seizes upon it and moves upward another rung on the ladder of success. It never occurs to him that he may fail. He sees only the opportunity, he visions what he can do with it, and all the forces within and without him combine to help him win. The unsuccessful man sees the same opportunity, wishes that he could take advantage of it but he is fearful that his ability or his money or his credit may be equal to the task. He is like a timid bather, putting in one foot and then drawing it swiftly back again - and while he hesitates some bolder spirit dashes in and beats him to the goal'. Who do you want to become? The choice is yours.

Opportunities are everywhere even in very difficult circumstances. Les Brown says, 'When hard times hit, we need to look for reasons to move forward, not for reasons to idle through life. When you don't move on life, life moves on you'. Most people see difficult times as a signal to stop moving. They do not realise that they need to take difficult times as a time to grow or consider turning their personal tragedies into a positive force for good in the world. People who seize the moment and learn from those moments have gone on and started successful charities after tragedies of the losing a loved one, for example. If you cannot change situations, it may be worth changing the way you view them. You have the power to turn the lemons in life into lemonade.

You have the power to live a better life and not a bitter life. So, associate with people who seize the opportunities to step into their greatness.

Are the people you associate with PRODUCTIVE with their time?

Great people are productive with their time. You and great people like Bill Gates have 24 hours in a day. Have you ever wondered why people have different levels of success within those 24 hours? To make you even wonder more, some people born 20 years after you and I have become more successful than us. What do they do differently? What have we done with our past 20 years? If we had our lives to live again, what would we do differently?

I think the first post-war Chancellor of Germany Konrad Adenauer gives us the answer, when he says, 'We all live under the same sky, but we don't all have the same horizon'. The poet Carl Sandburg adds, 'Time is the coin of your life. It is the only coin you have, and only you can determine how it will be spent. Be careful lest you let other people spend it for you'. People who have stepped into their greatness use their time differently. They know time is the new currency and they spend it wisely. They know that failing to plan their usage of time is planning to fail. While unsuccessful people waste time struggling to manage time, great people know that they cannot manage time, instead they manage themselves better with the time they have. So, the way you manage yourself in 24 hours makes the biggest difference.

Most people go through life with their weeks and days filled with a jumbled mess of activities. When they realise that they cannot do these activities effectively, they ask themselves:

Why me? Why is my life always in a mess? Why does trouble follow me wherever I go? Why is my life a major disaster? If people do not break this pattern of thinking and manage themselves and their emotions better, they end up living a roll-coaster life. To avoid this, one needs to be productive with their time. This will require prioritisation of tasks so that one is not overwhelmed. It means doing what is important so that one works smarter. It entails asking for help not because one is weak but because they want to remain strong. Wanting to do everything is setting oneself up to fail.

In effect, if you want to be productive with your time, you need to ask for help from the right people at the right time. It is necessary that you spend time on the things which matter to you. In the summer of 2017, I had a chance to go to the English countryside and camp with my family and friends. I had all the material necessary to pitch my tent but since I had not pitched a tent for some time, I asked one of my friends for help. My friend in turn asked for help from a 10-year-old boy who had acquired this skill from the Royal Air Force. He gave us the instructions, we followed them and our tent was up within 5 minutes. Why I am telling you this?

This is the reason. I had a tent but I was not sure how to pitch it. Sometimes, we want to be productive but we do not know how. I had poles to use in pitching my tent but was unsure how to erect them. Jim Rohn says, 'Success leaves clues'. It is necessary we ask for help from someone who has 'pitched their tents' before. Ask for help on how to be productive with your time not because you are weak but because you want to become more efficient. Ask for help not because you are selfish but because you want to give others the opportunity to serve you. Ask for help because in serving you, you give people the opportunity to express their greatness. Ask for help so that you are more productive than without the help.

Do the people you associate with LIVE FULL?

Great people live full and die empty. People who live full do not operate in the survival zone. They refuse to live a life that is below their potential as the greatness within them pushes them to say, 'There is something within me that says I can do better than this'. They do not settle for less than they are. They refuse to work to survive but work to thrive. They seek to connect with who they are. They use all they are and all they have to live full and die empty.

It is necessary for you to take time and think - if you had your life to live over again, what would you do differently? As you step into your greatness, seek to connect with yourself so that you live to the fullest. Do not live like a happy prisoner in your body. If you are a prisoner, be an unhappy prisoner. Stretch yourself beyond your prison and look for the exit to your best life. Remember that there are no limits when you are pursuing your greatness.

Great people know they cannot help others if they are not living a full life. Ona Brown famously known as the Dream Queen says, 'You can't pull out anything out of an empty bag'. This means you can only get from a bag that has something in it. As a result, great people fill themselves up first so that they can share with others from the overflow. As you seek to connect with great people, look for those who are full and drink from their overflow of greatness. If you continue drinking from people who are empty, you are likely to become emptied by them. They will suck all that you have left in you and you will become empty. So, find people who are overflowing with greatness. May their greatness become your daily drink so that you too live full.

Are the people you associate with EXEMPLARY?

This is the last feature of great PEOPLE. Great people live as examples. They are the message they bring. So, are the people you associate with good examples for you to follow? When you are going on an unfamiliar journey, it is helpful to go with someone who knows the way. Do the people you associate with know the way to your destination? Are they Satnavs for you to navigate you through all the corners of life to your dreams? Are they your life support system when you run out of oxygen? Do they pump you when you run out of pressure? Les Brown says supportive and exemplary people are 'not the people you pick along the way. These are people who pick you up along the way'. As you step into your greatness, be on the lookout for people who pick you along the way, who are seeing things for you, who are believing in you and in your greatness. Great people are always there to serve you. They know that you have something special. There is greatness within you.

Final Reflection

You have now completed the penultimate step to greatness. Before you move on to the final step, take time and reflect on the people you associate with. Ask yourself the following questions. What are they bringing into my life? Are they P.E.O.P.L.E©? In other words, are they: Purposeful? Encouraging? Opportunity experts? Productive? Living full? Exemplary? Do they fuel or empty my life? Do they empower me? Do they inspire me to become the best version of me? Do they enlighten my mind and ignite my heart? Ask yourself more and more questions - what am I becoming emotionally, academically, financially, and spiritually because of these people? Are there people who I need to upgrade or offload?

Before you go to the final step to greatness, go with PEOPLE and with all that you have learnt about PEOPLE. Go with the willingness and determination to be a PEOPLE too. Be purposeful with your life. Be encouraging no matter what happens. Be an opportunity expert. Be productive with your time. Live full. Be an example and a message of a great PEOPLE.

*Before moving on to the next step, complete the activities for **STEP 6** in the accompanying workbook titled '7 Steps to Greatness: The Workbook to Take Your Life, Studies, Career and Business to the Next Level'.*

STEP 7: Take Massive Action

'The path to success is to take determined, massive action'. Tony Robbins

Welcome to the last step to your greatness. It is amazing to notice how far you have come from. In this final step, we will focus on taking massive action and how this can keep you on the road to greatness. In my personal experience, A.C.T.I.O.N© is the difference between success and failure. People are great because they take A.C.T.I.O.N© so that their lives become a masterpiece. A.C.T.I.O.N© stands for:

- Ask questions

- Courageous

- Take risks

- Inspired by affirmations

- Obsessed with hope

- Never give up

Ask Questions

Great people ask questions. Like the world's number one life coach Tony Robbins, great people know that 'successful people ask better questions, and as a result, they get better answers'. Like the motivational speaker I heard some time back, great people know that 'life is a question and how you live it is the answer'. So, they decide to live their lives as a question. They ask questions related to their vision because they know that 'where there is no vision people perish'. They ask: Who am I? Why am I here? What brought me to this planet? What is the purpose of my life? What is my personal mission? How will future generations know that my life was worth living?

Like Les Brown, great people are aware that 'The graveyard is the richest place on earth, because it is there you will find all the hopes and dreams that were never fulfilled, the books that were never written, the songs that were never sung, the inventions that were never shared, the cures that were never discovered; all because someone was too afraid to take that first step, keep with the problem or determined to carry out their dream'. Great people ask questions related to their personal mission, dreams and goals. They ask - What is the dream for my life? Am I busy living my dreams or dying with my fears? What is it that I want to be my unique contribution to this world? What is my legacy?

Like Napoleon Hill, great people know that 'what the mind of man can conceive and believe, it can achieve'. They thus ask questions about the best way to conceive what they want. They study other people and ask - How can I use my imagination? What is the purpose of the movie I am playing on the screen of my mind? How can I put the power of my mind to work? How can I change the movie on the screen on my mind and be successful?

Like Porter Gale, great people know that your network is your net worth. They thus review their relationships and ask - Is this relationship purposeful? Is it encouraging? Does it give me the opportunity to meet with experts? Is it a productive use of my time? Is this relationship helping me to live full and die empty? Is it allowing me to have a good example to follow?

Self-education gives you a fortune

Searching for answers to these questions sets them on the road to self-education. The famous motivational speaker Jim Rohn says, 'Formal education will make you a living; self-education will make you a fortune'. Education is the key to becoming a better and committed builder of your masterpiece. As you might already know, the world is full of negative information that we feed our minds. For example, when you switch on any news channel, more than half of the news is negative. The media often covers bad news for example war in various countries, stock markets crashing, repossessions, economic depression on the way, crime rates up, deaths, suicide rates increasing, and many other areas. Even our social networking websites are cluttered with poor quality information. When I was growing up, there was only one day when we could be misled, 1st April, well known as April Fool's Day. Today, every day is a fooling day, especially with the explosion of fake news.

Imagine feeding your body with toxic and poor diet. How will it become? What about not feeding your body at all? What might be the consequences? Just as your body will become malnourished, starved, dehydrated and with the imminent possibility of death, it makes sense that you apply this to your mind too. If you feed your mind with toxic information, it will become toxic. This toxic information will spread and infect your heart as well. Imagine what will happen to the treasures buried in your heart! What will happen to your miracle power? What will happen to your gifts? What will happen to your greatness? They too will become infected.

Avoid toxic education

People who are stepping into their greatness avoid toxic education. They seek, find and use quality education that is the best medicine for their minds. They read books that become healthy foods for their bodies. When they achieve their greatness, they continue feeding their minds as they do not want to starve their greatness. Indeed, great people do not stop learning when they reach their greatness. By its very nature, greatness has no limits.

If you do not feed your mind with quality education, it will cost you. I remember I had a power cut in my apartment. I called an electrician to come and fix it. He came and within 5 minutes he had diagnosed the problem and had the power to fix the problem within 5 minutes. Given that he was greedy, he wasted time and it costed me £450 in less than 60 minutes. When I asked him what the problem was, he told me that the power had tripped due to a piece of equipment we had plugged in. All I needed was to reset the RCD! If I had educated myself on what to do, it wouldn't have costed me this much!

A quote attributed to the former president of Harvard University Derek Bok goes, 'If you think education is expensive, try ignorance'. In this case, ignorance costed me £450 which was a lot of money. The American President Benjamin Franklin says, 'If a man empties his purse into his head, no one can take it away from him. An investment in knowledge always pays the best interest'.

Programme your mind for greatness

As you take this final step, empower yourself with good quality education. Good education is the best food on the journey to your dreams, to your goals, and ultimately to your greatness. Good education programes your mind for greatness. My parents did not read what Benjamin Franklin wrote about education. However, they knew the value of good education and emptied their purses into our heads. This was their way of answering the questions they were facing at that time. I believe they faced questions such as, what is the best way out of poverty? What is the road to financial freedom? What is the legacy we are leaving our children? They knew that it is not what you leave your children that matters but what you leave in them. Our parents are leaving us good education as their legacy. They know that if we use this education well, we are able to make our life a masterpiece. In effect, feed your mind with good quality education for it programmes your life for greatness.

If you stop programing your mind for greatness with good education, your mind will be programed by life. You will not have the power to change the world. Instead the world will change you. Nelson Mandela says, 'Education is the most powerful weapon you can use to change the world'. Use education to change your life and the world. Use education to kill the fear within you so that you can dream big. Use education to stop the war inside and outside of you so that you become an instrument of peace. Use education to starve the poverty within you so that you manifest your greatness.

Education is an important investment you can make in yourself. Bill Gates, one of the world's richest person says, 'I really had a lot of dreams when I was a kid and I think a great deal of that grew out of the fact that I had a chance to read a lot'. Like Bill Gates, growing up I had many dreams and most of them have been realised because of the good education I received. One of my dreams was to fight poverty, so I educated myself and become a missionary, spending 10 years fighting material and immaterial poverty in my own family and in various parts of the world - Tanzania, Rwanda, Kenya, Burkina Faso, Algeria, France and England. So, keep asking questions and seeking answers on the best ways to live your dreams. When growth is guaranteed, don't settle. Continue investing in your personal spiritual, health, and financial education. Seek great PEOPLE and learn from them. One of the things you must learn is courage.

Courage

Great people go into action with courage. As you step into your greatness, you will definitely be in battle with your past. It will take you courage to face your past and accept who you are becoming today. It will take you courage to change and become the person you want to be from this day forward. Fortify yourself and know that your courage will come from within you and drive you into action fearlessly.

Be fearless

Great people know that courage is the key to taking control of one's life and face life's challenges. Like the inspirational British Prime Minister Winston Churchill, they admit that 'courage is the capacity to go from failure to failure without losing enthusiasm'. They know that your body cannot go to the West if your mind is travelling to the East. They realise that you cannot be successful if you spend most of your time focusing on failure. You can only go in the direction you travel. Effectively, great people develop the courage to focus on success for 'there is no philosophy which will help a man to succeed when he is always doubting his ability to do so and thus attracting failure' (Robert Collier). So, focus on success for when you are pursuing your greatness, failure is not an option. While some people fear failure, others fear success. In order to be successful, you need to face both failure and success without fear.

Fear is the number one killer of dreams. Fear steals our peace. Fear stops us from getting on in life. Fear makes us get involved in negative self-talk – 'I can't do it. I am not good enough'. Fear hinders us from taking action. When fear takes over, we sit in the back seat and do not know where we are going to end up. Sometimes we make fear bigger than us and it takes over our lives. We thus become afraid of making mistakes as we step into our greatness.

There will be times when you will fear and therefore not make a commitment. You will listen to your negative inner voice and conversation and these will hold you back. Not everyone will support you. Not everyone will be happy with your dream. Not everyone will encourage you to continue. Even some of your closest friends will become your great discouragers. The universe will seem to be turning against you. Your life will feel like an ongoing war characterised by unpredictable explosions, landmines, insecurities, and fears. It is during these moments that you will need to stand up within yourself against fear and say 'It is not over until I win'.

My advice is not to choose to be a permanent victim of fear in your life. There is a lot you can do to overcome it. In tough times, you must strengthen what is left in your heart. To persevere in such times, call upon your deepest purpose for support. Search deeper and find that voice within you that is saying 'whatever you desire is possible'. Let this voice give you the power to become fearless. Let it direct you to the best version of you. Let it lead you to your ultimate goal. When people see your resolve to fight until you win, they will then be attracted you. They will see you alive, enthusiastic, and courageous as you pursue your dreams. They will hear you say, 'I am standing to life and to its challenges. I have got what it takes. If I am going through hell, I will keep going. I will never give up on my dream. I will do whatever it takes. It is not over until I win'. You will be their example of a committed person and they will share from your overflow.

Commit to commitment

Allow me to ask you two questions - How many people do you know who talk a lot but achieve little? How many people do you know talk less and achieve a lot? The difference between them is commitment. In order to realise your personal mission, you need to be committed. In order to live your dreams, you need to be committed. In order to achieve your goals, you need to be committed. In order to step into your greatness, you need to be committed. Commitment is the vehicle which will drive you from vision into action and from dreams to reality. The philosopher Socrates said 'an uncommitted life is not worth living'. Then the genius Johann Wolfgang von Gothe wrote,

> *Until one is committed there is hesitancy, a chance to draw back…There is one elementary truth- the ignorance of which kills countless ideas and splendid plans. This is, that the moment one definitely commits oneself, then Providence moves too. All sorts of things*

occur to help one that would never otherwise have occurred. A whole stream of events issues from the decision, raising in one's favour all manner of unforeseen incidents and material assistance, which no man could have dreamed would have come his way. Whatever you can do or dream you can, begin it. Boldness has genius, power and magic in it, begin it now.

Until one is committed, life is not worth living. Allow your commitment to show up in A.C.T.I.O.N©:

- **A**sking questions

- being **C**ourageous

- **T**aking risks

- using **I**nspired affirmations

- being **O**bsessed with hope, and

- in **N**ever giving up.

What are you acting on now? Dr Norman Vincent Peale says, 'Be committed, to do what it takes, to have what you want'. Commitment will keep you on track to achieving what you want from life. I know this is true because I experienced it when I was doing my PhD between 2010 and 2015. Commitment allowed to stay on the track as I needed a clear picture of where I was going or else with two children, two jobs, one business, and doing a PhD, it would have been easy to fall off track.

Whatever you do, do it with commitment at all times. So, when you decide to take life on, do it with commitment. Someone said life is like an onion with many layers. You peel off one layer at a time and sometimes you cry. When you are committed, you become more aware that life has more than one layer. You are able to peel life one layer at a time. As you peel life, you are able to smile as well as cry. You will approach layers that will be hard to peel. Given that you are committed, you will continue to peel the many layers of life because you know it is not over until you reach the core. It is only at the core of life that you will find answers to the question which is your life. So, stay committed and run your life rather than running away from life. This involves risk.

Take Risks

Great people are risk-takers because they know that they would rather risk and get one percent from life than not risk and get zero percent from life. They also know that failing to risk is a risk. Like Helen Keller they admit that 'life is a daring adventure or it is nothing at all'. Shakti Gawain helps us visualise this adventure in her book *Creative Visualization*:

> *Let us imagine that life is a river. Most people are clinging to the bank, afraid to let go and risk being carried along by the current of the river. At a certain point, each person must be willing to simply let go, and trust the river to carry him along safely. At this point, he learns to "go with the flow" and it feels wonderful. Once he has become accustomed to being in the flow of the river, he can begin to look ahead and guide his own course onward, deciding where the course looks best, steering the way around boulders and snags, and choosing which of the many channels and branches of*

the river he prefers to follow, all while still "going with the flow"…Going with the flow means holding onto your goals lightly…and being willing to change them if something more appropriate and satisfying comes along. It is that balance between keeping your destination clearly in mind and yet enjoying all the beautiful scenes you encounter along the way, and even willing to change your destination if life starts taking you in a different direction. In short, it means being firm, yet flexible (p 58).

I am sure you have taken a lot of risks in your life. Even waking up creates a risk since you can fall stepping from your bed. Eating food creates a risk as you might choke. Crossing the road increases risk as you may get run over. I am reminded of a story that is often told in Tooro Kingdom in Uganda about a woman who knew the day when death was coming to her village. She decided not to go anywhere and stayed home so that death did not catch her. But she got bored and liking knitting, she got her thread and needle and started to knit. At one point she wanted to adjust the cloth she was knitting and put the needle into her mouth. When the cloth she was adjusting fell, she accidentally fell with it, swallowing the needle and died. This story teaches us that even when we plan to be risk free, risk can still find us.

Also be aware that there may be toxic people in your life. These people might always be negative, argumentative, and toxic to you. It is going to be a risk offloading them from your life if they are your friends. Instead of trying to change them, you will choose to change your friends. Remember, people are always pouring into you or taking out of you. Les Brown says, 'Being able to break away from toxic friendship can make the difference between living your dreams or living a nightmare'. You need to delete toxic people from your life. You need to upgrade your relationships so that you upload great people who will pour greatness into you.

Inspired Affirmations

Great people use inspiring affirmations which are verbalisations of their inner dialogue. Inner dialogues are likely to happen when the mind and the heart are talking to themselves during meditation, reflection and other moments of serenity. Some of the affirmations or inner dialogues can be negative and involve self-defeating thoughts. For example, 'Everything I do never works. Wherever I go problems follow me. I can't do this. This is never going to work for me'. This is negative mind talk.

Great people do not entertain negative mind talk. They consciously use inspired affirmations that are positive. Here are some of positive affirmations you can use:

- I create what I want in my life.

- I deserve to be happy and fulfilled.

- Every day in every way I'm getting better and better.

- I am the master of my life and creator of my destiny.

- Everything I need is already within me.

- Perfect wisdom is in my heart.

- I am whole and complete in myself.

- I love and appreciate myself just as I am.

- I accept all my feelings as part of me.

- There more I love myself, the more I give to others.

- I am attracting loving relationships into my life.

- My relationship with… is growing happier every day.

- I now have a satisfying and well-paid job.

- I communicate clearly and effectively.

- This is an abundant world and there is a lot for us.

- The more I give, the more I receive, the happier I feel.

- I feel happy just being alive.

- I am healthy and beautiful.

- The greatness within me is creating miracles in my life.

- I give thanks now for my life of health and happiness.

- I can do everything with Christ who strengthens me.

- My God is guiding me in everything that I do.

- God lives in me and manifests through me.

- The light of God surrounds me, the love of God enfolds me, the power of God flows through me.

- Wherever I am, God is, and all is well.

Remember, you can do affirmations silently or verbally, write them down or sing them. Choose what works for you. Affirmations need to be phrased positively and in the present. This acknowledges that they have already happened in your mind and what is left is making them happen materially.

Obsessed With Hope

One of the biggest challenges facing our world today is the shortage of hope. I remember being told a story about a town in Europe. Whereas people in the Western part of this town were affluent, those in the East were poor. Whereas people in the Western part of this town lived longer, those in the East had shorter lives. The main reasons people in the Western part were affluent and lived longer was because they had unlimited hope. They were obsessed with hope. The main reason people in the Eastern part were poor and lived shorter lives was because they had a shortage of hope.

As you step into your greatness and inspire others to do so, remember that people are failing to reach their greatness not because of the place they are born and not because of their career, gender or race. People are failing because of the size of their hope. While some people are unwilling to hope, others completely refuse to hope. My question to you is - what is the size of your hope? Are you ready to measure the size of your hope? Are you willing to increase the size of your hope to greatness? What are you willing to do or change after reading this book so that you increase your hope? I leave you with the words I heard from Pope Francis in 2017, 'Hope does not disappoint. Hope is sure. Be men and women of hope'. If you want to be great, increase the size of your hope. This will allow you to never give up.

Never Give Up or Give in

In life there are going to be moments when you going to say, 'I've had it'. These are the moments when you know that whatever you are doing is not in line with your purpose and is derailing you from your dreams and goals. These are the moments when you know that if you continue doing, staying or working where you are, you are destroying yourself. These are the times when you are not going to tolerate injustice in your life. These are the moments when you are going to leave the old you and walk towards the new you.

In these moments, taking A.C.T.I.O.N© will mean letting your fears go. In these moments, you need to call upon the hope within you and resolve to never give up. In times like these, never giving up will mean that you are determined to reset the clock and look for answers to your new life elsewhere. Once the universe notices your relentlessness to never give up, it will allow you to step into your greatness.

Let me leave you with the story of the builder that I heard from a famous speaker. It touched me and I remember it whenever I am in a situation that requires me to not give up:

> *There was a man who was an efficient builder. He had worked for years in a large company for many years and reached the age of retirement. His employer asked him to build one more house. It was to be his last commission. The builder took the job but his heart was not involved. He used inferior materials. Timber was poor. He failed to see them many things that should have been clear to him had he shown normal interest in his work. When the house was eventually finished his employer came to him and said the house was yours. Here is the key. The builder immediately regretted that he had used the worst materials and engaged the most incapable of workers. If only he had known that the house was for him.*

If the builder had made a commitment with his life to not give up until his last day on the job, if he had made a resolute decision that he was going to give it his best, he would have appreciated the gift.

As you step into your greatness, I do not wish you to be like the builder who gave up on the last days. Become a no matter what person. When you are a no matter what person, you set high standards for yourself all the time. When people hear your story and see you as someone who never gives up, they should be able to say 'Because of you I am not giving up. Because of you, I am alive today. Because of you, I am stepping into my greatness'. This is my story and I am ready to live my greatness.

LIVE YOUR GREATNESS

'I believe in you. I believe in your dreams. Live as a masterpiece because you are a piece of the master'.
Dr Patrick Businge

Congratulations you have completed the *7 Steps to Greatness.* What a journey you have made by climbing these steps. Now, let us look back and see what has happened on your journey and how you have grown.

On the first step, you had the chance to search and find yourself. You now know that you are a miracle in manifestation. You are uncommon and unrepeatable. You are gifted with greatness. With this self-knowledge, your life has taken on a new meaning and your eyes are opened to see a new horizon. But you did not stop there. You went on to take the second step.

In the second step, you took time to discover your purpose in this immense universe. You searched within yourself and found what you desired most. You found your why for living. You are now guarding what you have found like the apple of your eye. But you did not stop there. You took the next step.

In the third step, you allowed your purpose to give birth to your wildest dreams. You took James Dean's advice and were able to dream as if you will live forever. Dreaming while you were awake allowed you to discover your earliest dreams. Your dreams were big dreams because you knew from James Allen that dreamers were the saviours of the world. Your big dreams made you step out of your comfort zone and you have been able to witness defining moments unfold in your life. But you did not stop there. You took the next step.

In the fourth step to greatness, you learnt a unique set of goals – **S.T.A.R**© goals. You felt them strongly in your heart and connected them to your dreams. And as they occurred in the theatre of your mind, you were able to visualise them. While they became absolutely necessary to you, they have become a life and death issue too. You also set goals that were ridiculously hard to achieve because like Dr Norman Vincent Peale, you knew you were shooting for the moon and not the stars. This is because you became aware that when you begin stepping into your greatness, the process is more important than the outcome. But you did not stop there. You took the next step.

In the fifth step, you were able to see your dreams and your goals. You used the **V.I.S.I.O.N**© as the vehicle to go into another hemisphere with a different time zone where your contemplated your dreams. You **V**isualised **I**nside your mind with your **S**enses and **I**magined **O**vercoming obstacles with **N**o fear. This system allowed you - inside your mind - to have what you wanted. You realised that it was better to live from your imagination and not your memory. You overcame obstacles because you were now living from a place of FAITH and not of FEAR. You created a vision-board where you displayed your vision, your dreams and goals. But you did not stop there. You walked to the penultimate step.

In the sixth step, you contemplated on what Porter Gale said that your network is your net worth. You, thus, dedicated your time to reviewing your network using the **P.E.O.P.L.E**© model. You asked questions about the people you associated with: What were they bringing into my life? Were they purposeful? Encouraging? Opportunity experts? Productive? Living full? Exemplary? You went deeper and asked more questions: Did they fuel or empty my life? Did they inspire me to become the best version of me? Did they inspire my mind and ignite my heart? Did they empower me? What was I becoming emotionally, academically, financially, and spiritually because of these people? Upon asking and answering these questions, you offloaded toxic people and uploaded great people into your life. But you did not stop here. You made the commitment and kissed the final step.

In the final step, you made an unwavering decision to take massive action. You refused to park your dreams on the motorway of life. You committed to follow the **A.C.T.I.O.N**© system. Using this system, you emulated great people and asked important questions about your life, your dreams, goals and vision. You left no question unanswered and embarked on the road to educate yourself because you knew education was food for the mind. You knew the value of feeding your mind with good quality self-education and were, more than ever, committed to doing whatever it took to have what you wanted.

Now that you have reached the last step, you do not have to stop moving. You have to double your speed as you cruise on the motorway to your greatness. There are no more steps for you. You are now very special. You are a miracle child. You are uncommon. You are gifted with greatness. You are in this universe for a purpose. You have lots of dreams within you. You have the power to use S.T.A.R© goals and live your dreams. Step into action now. Walk with faith and show the world that you are unstoppable. Manifest your gifts and demonstrate to your community that you are an asset and not a liability to them. Live full and die empty. I believe in you. I believe in your dreams. Go and live your life as a masterpiece because you are a piece of the master.

ABOUT THE AUTHOR

Born in a small village in Uganda, Dr Patrick Businge did not let his circumstances characterised by war and abject poverty become his standard. Following his dreams while believing that no condition was permanent, he took steps to raise above his circumstances and made greatness his benchmark.

Dr Patrick Businge has gone on to become the Founder of Greatness University: the world's first institution dedicated to discovering, unlocking, and monetising greatness in individuals and businesses. His main goal is to help you tap into your greatness faster and easily than you can ever imagine.

Dr Patrick Businge is an educator. He has taught over 50 000 people in classrooms, churches, orphanages, villages, community centres, and boardrooms throughout the United Kingdom of Great Britain, Europe, Africa, and the Americas.

Dr Patrick Businge is also a strong believer in lifelong learning and personal development. He has studied in over 7 universities and acquired over 10 postgraduate qualifications. He has researched, written and spoken for approximately 20 years in the fields of ethics, philosophy, religion, education, armed conflict, disability, and greatness. Living in a world characterised by war, plagued by a shortage of hope and marred with average performance, his ultimate vision is to inspire one million people become instruments of peace, messengers of hope and channels of greatness.

Dr Patrick Businge speaks to various audiences on Personal and Professional Development. His exciting talks, transformational seminars and life changing boot camps on 7 Steps to Greatness, Book Writing, Self-Esteem, STAR Goals, Success Mindset, and Finding Your Best Self bring about immediate change and long-term results.

Dr Patrick Businge has travelled and worked in over 10 countries on 3 continents. He speaks four languages: English, French, Swahili and some Arabic. Patrick is happily married and has 2 children. He is active in community and national affairs. To learn more about his programs, seminars and services, please visit www.greatness-university.com. If you have any personal questions email him directly at info@greatness-university.com or meet him on Facebook, Twitter, LinkedIn and Instagram.

BY THE AUTHOR

*7 Steps to Greatness: The **Masterplan** to Take Your Life, Studies, Career and Business to the Next Level*

*7 Steps to Greatness: The **Workbook** to Take Your Life, Studies, Career and Business to the Next Level*

*7 Steps to Greatness: The **Journal** to Take Your Life, Studies, Career and Business to the Next Level*

*7 Steps to Greatness: The **Seminar** to Take Your Life, Studies, Career and Business to the Next Level*

*7 Steps to Publish the Book in You: The **Retreat** to Discover, Write, Publish and Monetise your Book*

Greatness University: *Online courses at*

www.greatness-university.com

Author contact: info@greatness-university.com

7 STEPS TO GREATNESS SEMINARS

Most people are not living their dreams because they are living their fears. In this foundational training, you will deepen your awareness of the 7 steps that will take fear out of the process and turn your dreams into reality. You will learn the core strategies Dr Patrick Businge has learnt from his mentors like the world's number one motivational speaker Les Brown and has used in his path to greatness. These strategies will help you to live your dreams and cruise on the path to your greatness.

When you complete this course, you will:

- Discover the greatness within you

- Develop your mindset for greatness

- Create a formula on finding your purpose

- Design a three dimensional lifestyle

- Develop and use STAR goals

- Deliver your success like all great people.

You have something special. There is greatness within you. Everything you need to live a great life is within you. This training will give you strategies to access your greatness, inspire confidence in your mind, and ignite your heart to go after your dreams.

BOOK WRITING RETREATS

A lot of people want or have at least thought about writing a book. This is because there are a lot of benefits to having a book with your name on it. Writing a book and becoming a published author allows you to position yourself as an expert in your field, increase your credibility, share your message with the world and transform your business. However, few people ever write and publish their book. When you come to our retreat, you will discover that writing your book is not that complicated. We will give you a 7 step roadmap to write, publish and monitise your book. In this roadmap, you will get the strategies that we have acquired from our mentor: Brian Tracy, bestselling author of over 83 books, on how to:

- Discover the book within you

- Learn the blueprint to write and design your book

- Learn and develop the skills to become a great author

- Publish and promote your book

- Turn your book into a profitable business.

You have something special. There is a book within you. Come to our book writing retreats and discover, write, publish and monetise the book within you. Allow the world to read and be transformed by your message.

Greatness University

Greatness University was born out of the realization that we live in world where we are sold almost anything and everything except one important product: greatness. So, we decided to become the world's first institution dedicated to discovering, unlocking, and monetising greatness.

We believe greatness leaves clues. We are therefore committed to helping people like you tap into their greatness faster and easily than you can ever imagine. We do this by researching greatness in individuals, organizations, businesses, and other spheres of life. We help people like you create their own personal economies by monetising their greatness. We guide people like you on the best ways to create a lasting legacy. Remember, your legacy is not what you give to the people you love but what you will live in them.

At Greatness University, we partner with like-minded people to unlock greatness around the world. We offer online courses, run face to face training, give one to one mentoring, and organize boot camps in our areas of expertise worldwide. Our courses and mentoring in the Principles of Greatness, Setting STAR Goals, Live Your Dreams, Walk in Greatness, The Millionaire in You, Speak and Change the World, and Discover the Book in You are not only focused on developing your mind but also speaking to your heart: where your treasure is.